❝ There's more to the hiring process than just posting an ad, picking out a few good résumés, interviewing several people, and making an offer. It's a process that requires some planning if you want to make the best hire possible. But it doesn't have to be an over-whelming task if you break it down into small steps and give yourself enough time to work your way through each one. **❞**

BARNES & NOBLE

MANAGEMENT
BASICS™

HIRING

BY C. J. PRINCE

**BARNES
& NOBLE
BOOKS**
NEW YORK

Foreword

As a manager, you need to ensure you get the right person for the job. To do that you need to have a hiring process in place that covers all the vital steps, from hammering out a solid job description to making an offer. In *Hiring*, the first book in the new Barnes & Noble Management Basics™ series, that process is revealed in easy-to-follow language that shows you how to find your next hire like a pro.

It starts with assessing your hiring needs so that the job description really does match the job and can then serve as a safety net to sift through the resumes you'll receive. You'll see how to create a criteria checklist to simplify the work of phone screenings and basic reference checks. When you have zeroed in on the right candidates, you'll learn how to manage that first interview to reveal each candidate's skill sets, as well as personality type and attitudes.

You'll also find expert tips on checking references and how to use that information during the second interview to help inform your final decision. There are also guidelines on making an offer, upping the ante if necessary, and then sealing the deal.

And the advice doesn't stop there. *Hiring* takes you one step further and shows you how to make your new employee's first days productive and enjoyable.

So turn the page and take the anxiety out of the hiring process. Believe it or not, you'll emerge from the hiring process a better manager, and with great hires to show for it!

Wynn Madrigal
Editorial Director
Barnes & Noble Management Basics™ series

TABLE OF CONTENTS

CHAPTER ONE

THE HIRING LANDSCAPE

The benefits

You have finally been given the green light to hire! Good for you. It means that senior management trusts your judgment enough to make the right choice. And you will. Don't be put off by those who say that hiring is a full-time job. It isn't. All you need to do is break down the hiring process into time-specific tasks. Even if you have never hired before, you can manage the entire process—from writing (or rewriting) the job description, to screening and interviewing, to choosing someone and making a job offer.

The good news is that going through a systematic hiring process can teach you a lot about your company and your department. Moreover, it will teach you a lot about yourself as a manager.

Best of all, making a hire gives you a great opportunity to analyze the way your team is structured and investigate changes to boost productivity or gain efficiency. You'll also have an opportunity to gain valuable insights from other employees as well as other managers about the way they organize their staff and team members.

ASK THE EXPERTS

What if I've never hired before?

That's okay—every manager has to make a first hire. The key is not to become overwhelmed by the desire to make "the perfect hire." There is no such thing. What you're aiming for is a **high-probability hire**—someone who has all or the majority of the skills you are looking for, is likely to accept a job offer from you, and is likely to stay with the company long term and make a solid contribution. The way you make a good hire is by staying organized, listening carefully, asking the right questions, and, above all, remembering that the hiring process is an opportunity for both you and your prospective applicants to learn.

FIRST PERSON INSIGHTS
A blessing in disguise

"When I was promoted to manager, I wound up having to hire someone my first month on the new job. I was terrified both that my own work would suffer due to the extra time I would be spending on the hiring process, and that I might choose the wrong person and prove myself incompetent. But the process wound up being a lot more useful than I thought it would be to my new job. Developing the job description, for example, gave me insight I would otherwise not have had into one of the jobs I was managing and also allowed me to handpick the kinds of skills that ultimately would make my job easier. I also learned a lot about myself through the process. Today, when I have to hire—believe it or not—I actually enjoy it."

Vijay S., Naperville, IL

The challenge

It's a lot of work—but well worth the effort

On the face of it, hiring seems like it should be a simple enough task. You advertise the job and have your pick of the qualified candidates who come running. You ask a few pointed questions, and the moment the perfect candidate emerges, you hire that person, integrate him or her into the corporate culture and—poof!—the gap in your team is filled and you can immediately begin reaping the benefits of the talent you found.

Ah, if only it were that simple. What is nearly always the case is that you need to hire someone quickly. You have to replace a key employee who is suddenly leaving, be it to go back to school or take a new job. Or your department has been given so much work all of a sudden that you have to hire someone to help out now. Whatever the case, you'll have to kick into high gear to hire top talent for your team.

Are you worried that you won't have the time to hire? For starters, you need to realize that you are not alone. There are a number of resources you can turn to.

Most companies with over 50 employees have a human resources department; for more on this see pages 18–19. Large companies also often have established relationships with outside recruiters; for more on their role, see pages 20–21.

If you work for a small company with no official human resources department, don't fret. Typically, at small companies, there are one or two managers who have done most of the company's hiring. They were the ones who, no doubt, hired you. Get in touch with them to ask for their guidance.

WHAT IF?

What if my manager isn't sure whether the job is a full-time or part-time position?

In those cases, you need to assess exactly what you need to have done on a year-round basis. Companies whose business is seasonal will have different personnel needs throughout the year. For example, a retailer who sells children's toys will need to staff up at Christmas time. Some managers will ask you to hire a part-time person to cut costs, though this is not always the most effective decision in the long run, and may lead to higher turnover costs. Part-time employees might be tempted to jump ship the moment a full-time job becomes available elsewhere, and such employees often don't develop a "team spirit" or loyalty to the organization. There are other options to consider, such as hiring people on a project basis. These are called **contingency hires**. For more on this type of worker, see pages 202–203.

What if my manager isn't convinced we need to replace the employee we lost—but I am. How do I make my case?

Particularly when times are tight, management will see an employee's departure as an opportunity to re-allocate that individual's workload and eliminate the position. To convince them otherwise, you'll have to submit a document detailing the work the departed employee was responsible for, estimating the time each task takes per work week, and outlining the workloads of other employees to illustrate why they can't take on the additional tasks.

Either you'll discover, to your own surprise, that the department can survive with fewer people after a bit of reshuffling, or you'll make your case, and, in the process, develop a rough job description to which you'll be able to refer when it comes time to advertise.

The hiring process

There's more to the hiring process than just posting an ad, picking out a few good résumés, interviewing several people, and making an offer. It's a process that requires some planning if you want to make the best hire possible. But it doesn't have to be an overwhelming task if you break it down into small steps and give yourself enough time to work your way through each one. Here's a quick look at the main steps in the hiring process:

Take stock of what you need. Meet with HR or recruiters to talk about the kind of employee you are looking for and what you can offer.

Prepare or update the job description (see pages 38–43), your hiring criteria, and your hiring budget (see pages 36–37).

Research salaries for this job and the current job market. Rectify any gaps between your hiring budget and the salary range (see page 36).

Write an ad for the job, print it in selected newspapers and/or post online (see pages 48–52).

Begin screening résumés (see pages 70–71) and doing basic background research on applicants that fit the job criteria (see pages 80–84).

Conduct phone screening interviews with the top candidates (see pages 72–73) to narrow down the list for in-person interviews.

Interview your top candidates and test if applicable (see page 76).

Check references (see chapter 9) to help you narrow your search again to the top two or three candidates.

Do second-round interviews with the top candidates (see pages 134–135).

Make an offer to your top choice and close the deal (see page 168).

Welcome your new employee on board! (See chapter 11.)

YOUR HIRING TIMELINE

Naturally, no one timeline will work for every situation, given that sometimes you will have to fill a position quickly. But if you have plenty of advance notice, then an ideal hiring timeline might look like this:

Two to three months before the start date

■ Determine your hiring needs (see page 28) and create or review the job description (see pages 40-43).

■ Determine your hiring budget and set a salary range (see pages 34-37).

■ Talk to your HR department to see how it can help you with the process. If you plan to use job recruiters, start investigating firms (see page 20).

■ Start considering your advertising options (see page 48).

Six to eight weeks before start date

■ Hire a recruiter if necessary.

■ Decide on the type and amount of advertising you want to do.

■ Write the job ad and post it online and/or print it in selected media.

■ Examine your schedule and block out time for scanning resumes.

■ Begin screening resumes and pick out a few good possibilities .

Four to six weeks before start date

■ Conduct phone screening interviews to narrow your choices down.

■ Schedule in-person interviews.

Three to four weeks before start date

■ Do early reference checking if possible.

■ Conduct round-one and round-two interviews.

Two to three weeks before start date

■ Check references carefully.

■ Decide on your top pick and get approval if necessary.

■ Make a formal offer of employment and start salary negotiations.

■ Reach an agreement and provide an employment letter or contract.

■ Notify other applicants that the position has been filled.

Managing the process

Why you need an organized approach

Too often, managers hire one of the first few candidates or one of the last few they see because those are the ones they remember best. Of course, no one sets out to hire the wrong person. Yet poor hiring continues to plague companies at all levels—and most of the time, the failures are a result of insufficient planning up front or inconsistency in following the various steps in the process. While there are clever candidates out there who will oversell themselves by inflating their own skills or abilities, most can be caught and weeded out by the right interview questions and solid reference checking.

That means staying organized every step of the way. When the résumés do start coming in, it's going to be a lot to keep track of, particularly once the interviewing gets under way. You may be impressed with a candidate at the time of the interview, but a few days—and a dozen interviews—later, he or she may be just a blur. By keeping meticulous, organized notes about each candidate, you exponentially increase your chances of making a better decision.

Getting the hiring process down to something of a science will also enable you to show your best side to prospective employees. Their first encounter with the company is through you; coming across as organized and respectful immediately gets you off on the right foot and ensures a good working relationship and a positive attitude.

GETTING ORGANIZED

1. Create a job folder to keep track of your materials.

2. Put into the folder all the info you've collected about the job, such as the job description, and all the correspondence with human resources and recruiting agencies.

3. Prepare blank sheets that allow you to fill in candidates' names, contact info. Make lots of copies. You'll attach these to each candidate's résumé. Later you'll add a separate sheet for reference checking.

If you prefer working electronically, there are several software packages that help manage the hiring process, including ACT!, Contact Plus, and GoldMine.

THE COST OF TURNOVER

One downfall of not being organized throughout the hiring process is that you can lose track of your best candidates and so run the risk of hiring the wrong person—and then having that person quit or be fired shortly afterward. This can result in a high **turnover rate**—the number of workers who leave over a given period of time divided by the total number of workers. And this can quickly rack up costs, both quantifiable and not-so-quantifiable, that hit directly at the bottom line of your company or department. As a result of high turnover, customers may experience disruptions in service and become unhappy with you. High turnover can also cost you valuable time. Undoubtedly, you had to carve out a significant chunk of your schedule the first go-round, including training the new hire. You don't want to have to do it again. So the bottom line is that you want to get it right the first time.

Working with HR

If your company has a Human Resource, or HR, department, you should contact them as soon as you get the green light to start the hiring process. There are several key things HR can provide for you:

■ EEOC information on hiring procedures. This is to make sure your hiring process reflects all the latest EEOC guidelines. For more on legal issues regarding hiring and interviewing, see pages 20–21.

■ Names and contact information of recruiters who can help with your search; see pages 20–21.

■ Previous job descriptions for the job you are hiring for; see pages 40-43.

■ Salary range information; see pages 34–35.

■ Internal posting procedures, if your company has an internal job posting site. There may be dozens of qualified applicants in your company right now who would like to make a change, not to mention employees looking to relocate to another state who would much prefer a job at another branch of your organization than one at a new company.

Find out if your HR department has a company Web site that allows employees to search for jobs by keyword as well as by country, state, and city. Some companies will use job alerts or weekly e-mails to notify interested employees of new openings in their field or location of interest. If so, make sure yours is listed with HR.

You should also check out your company's **personnel database** housing the résumés from employees who've applied to various jobs internally but, for one reason or another, were not hired for the position. Different departments may have different policies and rules for contacting employees; get the lowdown from HR before you contact anyone to set up an interview.

ASK THE EXPERTS

Should I designate a period of time for internal recruitment before opening it up to external candidates?

It depends on your company's policies. Some companies require that you post new job openings for a specific amount of time before advertising it to the public. If your company has this rule, then you need to factor that time into your hiring process.

Do I have to include salary in an internal job post?

Not necessarily. If wage listing is optional, per your company's posting procedures, then you don't have to—and probably shouldn't if you're not revealing salary in your external search. For some positions, however, including part-time and administrative jobs, your company may require at least a salary range. If the position is management-level, you can probably get authorization to say only that salary is commensurate with experience.

Using recruiters

Finding talented people to fill your job needs is hard. Especially since the best talent is often already employed. How do you find those people? One way is to hire an outside search firm, also known as **recruiters**, or **headhunters**. Recruiters have an established network of contacts in various industries that they can tap into to find employed candidates who might be looking for a change. Some recruiters specialize in technology, others in marketing, others in finance. So, since their value is in their connections, you'll want to work with a firm with a proven track record in your industry.

Using the services of a recruiting firm is expensive. There are different ways of paying for their services. Nearly all recruiters work on a **contingency** basis, meaning they charge a fee based on a certain percentage of the new hire's yearly salary, usually around 25 percent of that first year's total compensation. For example, if you are looking for a VP of operations for a salary of $90,000 and a signing bonus of $10,000, they will bill your company up to $30,000 if they get you the candidate.

Large companies that do a lot of hiring often have search firms on a yearly **retainer**. Such firms are still paid on a search-by-search basis, but they are also paid a monthly retainer fee to make themselves available for multiple searches. Retained firms usually focus on staffing higher-level positions and do exhaustive searches in which they weed out and vet only the most highly qualified candidates.

Since a headhunter will essentially be the link between you and prospective candidates—and therefore be a reflection of your company—he or she must be someone who will make the right impression. Qualities to look for include honesty, excellent communication skills, good understanding of the needs of the position and your industry, attention to detail, and a professional demeanor. The recruiter you interview should be able to provide several references, which you should check carefully.

ASK THE EXPERTS

I'm relying on the recruiter to find the right person, but shouldn't I do the salary negotiation myself? Doesn't the recruiter get a percentage of that salary?

It's tempting to do the negotiating yourself, but you're better off not doing it. Ultimately, the recruiter is working for you—and hopes to continue to work for you on many more searches in the future. His or her goal is not to bilk you out of money on one job. And since the recruiter is acting partly as career counselor for candidates—even though the recruiter is on your dime— he or she has the inside scoop on what the candidate really wants. The recruiter's job is to make sure both sides are happy and that you don't lose your candidate to another company's counteroffer.

QUESTIONS TO ASK BEFORE HIRING A RECRUITER

- How many successful searches have you personally conducted?

- How many in our industry?

- Have you conducted any searches for competitor companies?

- What is the average tenure of the employees you've placed?

- Would you walk me through your process for finding and hiring candidates, from job requisition to hire?

- How long do you estimate it will take until we can start interviewing?

- How do you measure your success rate? By number of candidates placed? Or by the number of candidates you have placed that have remained on the job for more than two years?

- What are your payment terms ?

Hiring internally

The politics of hiring internally

You've been noticing that a neighboring department has a star employee—intelligent, talented, always early for work, with a solid reputation in the business. He's just the kind of team player you'd like to have on your team. When a position suddenly opens up in your division, can you make any moves to solicit that employee?

Not really—unless your company encourages this. Those companies that do are the ones that ask employees during their evaluations if they have any relocation interests or desires to move into different areas of the company. If your company does foster this kind of open-ended career growth, then talk to the employee's manager and find out whether he or she has made such requests. That will, of course, alert that manager to your interest, but you wouldn't have been able to do anything without his or her approval anyway.

Some of the bigger companies, particularly those in the technology industry, have instituted employee **redeployment programs** to help downsized workers be redeployed within the company. That means that instead of being shooed out the door with a pink slip, they go into the pool of candidates for employment elsewhere in the organization. For companies who've been through a round or two of painful layoffs, redeployment programs are an effective way to boost morale and retain people in whom you've already sunk significant training resources. They also help to limit potential corporate liability during a massive downsizing. Find out from human resources whether such a program or anything like it exists in your company; if so, ask to be notified when employees are laid off in other departments under those circumstances.

ASK THE EXPERTS

But don't companies usually lay off the less talented employees first?

No. Very often a unit or division will be instructed to reduce head-count by a certain percentage and any number of factors will go into their decision making, including salary and reorganization of positions. Mergers, too, will force this kind of layoff situation, since the acquired company or division will introduce redundancies into the organization. In many cases, this gives you an opportunity to get first crack at talented, highly skilled employees who are eager to find work at the company.

Why would another manager be willing to lose a great employee to me?

Chances are he or she won't be thrilled, but the company usually dictates policy on this, and more and more often, companies are realizing it's better to lose an employee to another division within the company than to a competitor. On occasion, two managers will also arrange a "swap," or a trade, just as baseball managers do to round out one particular area of strength on the team. This kind of arrangement doesn't always present itself, but when it does, it's an effective way of introducing new talent without forcing turnover.

Promoting your own people

Consider promoting from within

Although most managers like to think they are grooming their people for advancement to higher levels in the organization, it can be difficult to picture them in a new job. Many managers are resistant to "losing" a talented person from a position he or she has excelled in. But talented employees who are ready to move up won't stick around forever. And if they see that you're not even considering promoting internally, it will discourage them from working toward advancement.

If a job opens up that would offer a promotion to someone on your team, make sure employees know about it. Just be careful not to pit people against each other for a promotion. Do not put forth your "favorites," and always try to remain as objective as possible.

There are several advantages to hiring from within. First, obviously, your hiring costs are lower, and you may also save on salary, as promotions tend to cost less than new hires. You also save on training and orientation costs, since you are hiring someone who is already very familiar with the company—its policies, procedures and so on. An existing employee is also a known quantity as far as how he or she will fit in with the team and get along with you personally, while a new employee—even one who impressed you in the interview—is still a wild card.

Finally, you improve morale across your team by following a culture of promoting from within. Companies with a reputation for recognizing and rewarding talent within their ranks are understandably in demand by talented workers.

ASK THE EXPERTS

I was thinking of promoting an outstanding performer in my group, but he does his current job so efficiently and skillfully—what if I can't replace him?

That's one of the main reasons managers fail to promote their top-performing employees. Unfortunately, they often lose that employee in the end, once he becomes sufficiently frustrated with the limitations of his position. Remember, your goal is to retain your best people. And great people stay at organizations that reward excellence. Apart from offering compensation and perks, the best way to reward an employee who performs well is to recognize that performance and advance him up the ladder. Best of all, you'll still have that person on board to help recruit and train the individual who later steps into that position.

INTERNAL CANDIDATES TRUMP EXTERNAL CANDIDATES

When it's a choice between an external job candidate who looks great on paper and interviews exceptionally well, and an internal candidate who is a solid performer, you may be better off with the latter, according to a 2002 study conducted by a group of researchers at the Cornell School of Hotel Administration. The study, entitled "How to Compare Apples to Oranges: Balancing Internal Candidates' Job-Performance Data with External Candidates' Selection-Test Results," found that past-performance appraisals are more valid in predicting future job performance than interviews, tests, and job simulations. This is particularly true for management and supervisory positions, but it is also valid for other types of employees, such as sales clerks, bank tellers, and production workers. So, according to this study, an employee who has already proven himself on the job may be a safer choice than a candidate whom you have never seen in action.

Helpful resources

BOOKS

Topgrading: How Leading Companies Win by Hiring, Coaching and Keeping the Best People
by Bradford D. Smart

Hire With Your Head: A Rational Way to Make a Gut Decision
by Lou Adler

Decision by Objectives: How to Convince Others That You Are Right
by Ernest Forman
and Mary Ann Selly

WEB SITES

These sites offer a comprehensive range of staffing metrics, articles, and other resources for HR execs and managers.

Staffing.org
www.staffing.org
A global nonprofit corporation, Staffing.org is designed to help site members enhance their staffing expertise and performance.

HR.com
www.hr.com
HR.com offers information on the full gamut of human-resources tasks, including a comprehensive section on hiring. Designed primarily for human-resources professionals, this site is a handy resource for any manager who has to hire.

The HR Chally Group
www.chally.com/turnover_cost_calculator.htm
Find out what the cost of turnover might be for various positions at your company with this calculator from the HR Chally Group.

CHAPTER TWO

GETTING STARTED

Fleshing out the job

Know what you're looking for

Hiring smart always starts with knowing what you want before you start looking. Sounds simple enough—yet far too often managers charged with hiring a new employee set out on the process (see page 14) without having really figured out exactly what skills they need. Getting a "motivated self-starter" or "someone with a good, positive attitude" is nice, but there's more to the job than that.

The more specific you can be up front about the skills, experience, and personality fit you're looking for, the better your chances of finding the right match. Start by putting aside any existing assumptions about the job, and ask yourself what your team needs in a new position. Is this a job or function you want to keep status quo, or does it need some tweaking? If you're replacing someone who didn't work out, why didn't they? Have you identified the reasons and now know which qualities made that person a wrong fit?

Involve your employees in this evaluation process by inviting them into your office for a one-on-one chat; get their input on what kinds of skills or experience is needed to round out the team. By doing this, you not only gain information about your internal processes, but you communicate to your other employees that you value their opinions and concerns. They will be far more motivated to help get the right person in place and, later, to help integrate the new employee into the culture. And that is something you can never have too much help with.

ASK THE EXPERTS

I'm responsible for hiring an employee who will be supervised by the manager just below me on the hierarchy. How can I ensure success?

This is fairly common in large companies. You can dramatically improve the chances of success by heavily involving the supervising manager up front, when you're clarifying the job description, required skills, and ultimate goals and expectations for the position. Ask that manager to submit a specific list of criteria and skills and an explanation of how he or she sees the job shaping up. Review it together and discuss any changes you want to make. While you are the one who is ultimately responsible for the final hiring decision, doing your best to make it a collaborative effort will go a long way toward ensuring a successful hire.

I was told to hire someone by senior management, but was given only vague direction. How can I ask for the guidance I need without looking incompetent?

The only incompetence is in not asking. Management needs to be clearer with you about the position they've conceived, and it's your job to probe them if they haven't let you in on it. Schedule a meeting with one or two of the executives who made the decision and let them know you want to be thorough. Gently force them to be as specific as possible by asking very detailed questions. Be sure to meet with any team members the new hire will be working with.

Replacing staff

When you are filling an existing job

When it comes to hiring, there are basically two possible scenarios: a) you will be hiring to fill a position vacated by an employee who has been promoted or transferred, or has left the organization, or b) you will be hiring to fill a newly created position (see page 32). These two scenarios require somewhat different hiring strategies.

If you are merely replacing staff, chances are you already have a good idea of what the job entails. And there may also be an existing job description (see page 40) for the position.

If you do have such a description already, or your HR department can provide one, this will simplify the hiring process because you will know exactly what to look for. However, that doesn't mean you should just turn the description into an ad, publish it in the local paper, and hope for the best. Review the description to make sure that it is still relevant and, even better, review it with the employee who is leaving the position to see how he or she thinks it should be modified.

If it hasn't been very long—say, up to six months—since the previous employee was hired for this position, you may even be able to go back to the other top candidates from the previous search, if there were any, and see if they are still interested in the position. This can cut down a lot on the number of new applicants you'll need to consider.

Finally, if you are merely replacing staff, a lot of your work may already be done when it comes to fixing a salary range (see pages 36–37). It may merely be a matter of updating the range used for the previous hire by taking into account inflation or cost-of-living increases since the old employee was hired. However, if you are hiring in a particularly volatile industry—in other words, one where the supply and demand for jobs changes quickly—you may need to do some additional salary research (see page 34) in order to find out what the best range is right now.

ASK THE EXPERTS

We need to get someone into this empty position very quickly, but the process isn't leaving me any time to work and I'm worried about my work suffering. What should I do?

The first thing to do, if you haven't already, is have a talk with your boss. Make him aware of what's involved in the hiring process (see pages 14–15 for an overview of this). List all the associated tasks and estimate the amount of time each takes you per day. This should help you make a case to hire temporary help, if that is what's needed, or to temporarily suspend your responsibilities or share them with another manager while you're busy hiring. Chances are your manager has hired before and is familiar with the time-consuming nature of it; he likely also understands the importance of making a careful, quality hire.

A brand-new job

When you're adding rather than replacing

If you've gotten the green light to staff up and add a new member to the team—congratulations! That's good news for you and your company. It means you are doing so well that you can add a salary without eliminating one.

It also means you have to hire for a position that didn't previously exist, which can be challenging, depending on whether the job is entirely new. If you're just adding to the sales team, for example, or adding an account manager to handle new customers, you can draw on existing job descriptions and criteria for those positions.

Hiring to add new skills or to achieve an entirely new goal, however, may require a bit more digging. If the decision to hire came from above, start there. Sit down with the executive or senior manager—and anyone else who may have been in on it—and flesh out the job criteria by asking questions such as: Who will this employee report to, and who will his coworkers be? What tasks will he be responsible for? What kinds of skills should he have in order to complement the skills of existing employees in the department? What kind of experience should he have?

Getting specifics becomes critical when you're interviewing for a position with which you're not at all personally familiar and have never done yourself. Here are some pointers:

- First, draw on internal resources. Find out if the position exists elsewhere in the organization, and if it does, call up the manager in that department to get his or her assessment of the most critical skills involved.

- Second, search the classifieds, both online and in print media, for descriptions of a similar job and note the key criteria. Remember, the candidates you'll be seeing will be trying to wow you; in order to sift the diamonds from the rest, you'll need to know how to evaluate them.

QUESTIONS TO ASK ABOUT STAFFING UP

Here are several questions you should ask the people who have made the decision to hire, or those who are familiar with the position you are trying to fill:

- Why are we adding this position?
- What specifically will be achieved if the match is right?
- What skills will the candidate need in order to succeed in this position?
- Do these skills require a specific degree?
- Is industry experience critical?
- Will this job overlap with any of the other jobs on the team? If so, have we thought about restructuring that position to gain greater efficiency?
- Who can I involve in the hiring process with the appropriate knowledge to help ensure that we hire the right person?

Salary ranges

Researching what the market will bear

Once you have a fairly clear idea about the job you want filled, the next step is to find out what the going salary is. You may already have a vague idea, but it is important to have up-to-date information.

Begin by checking with your HR department to find out if employees fitting a similar description have been hired recently. Depending on corporate policy, you may be able to get a summary of that employee's **compensation package** (the salary, benefits, and perks for a particular employee). You may have to get clearance from his or her manager first.

There are now a host of Web sites that offer general salary ranges for hundreds, if not thousands, of job titles in regions across the United States and around the world. (See page 46 for a list of sites.) If you want something less generic, you can purchase highly detailed salary reports with plenty of comparison data and accompanying charts and graphs. For example, at **www.SalaryExpert.com** you can get a detailed report for less than $40 that includes dozens of compensation variables to help you devise a fair package. This exercise will help you not only on the front end, but later on when it's time to negotiate salary.

Also remember that salaries can vary widely by region. If you are hiring for a position in a location other than the one in which you live and work, you need to be familiar with salary ranges for different cities. Just as an example, the median salary of a construction supervisor in California is around $57,000, while in Utah, it's about $40,000.

ASK THE EXPERTS

I now realize we need to offer more money for the position we're hiring for. But how can I convince my boss?

The best way is by showing the numbers from your salary research. By checking the classifieds and job boards in your region, you can also present salary ranges offered by competitors for the same position. Draft a memo that includes this research as well as the potential cost of turnover for that position, including training and recruiting costs. If you can show that losing that person to a better offer later will cost more than increasing the offer now, you have made a good case. Even if your manager doesn't come around, you have offered your opinion, in writing, and no one will blame you later if the new hire isn't successful.

Can I cut back on salary in a down market, when unemployment is higher?

When more people are out pounding the pavement, you can usually hire for less than what you'd pay in a strong economy. And chances are your budget will be tighter during that time anyway. But keep in mind that the cost of living doesn't usually go down all that much even when the economy goes south, and, as they say, what goes down eventually goes up. Make sure you're not that far off salarywise, so your gifted employee won't be tempted to jump ship when the tide turns. What you should be most concerned with is keeping in step with what your competitors are paying, since they are vying for the same talent.

We don't have any direct competitors locally. Do I still need to worry about paying well?

Could you get away with it if your employees seemingly have nowhere else to go? Yes. Would you want to? Probably not. Remember, the goal is to have happy, productive employees who will then go out and delight your customers with their enthusiasm. To get the fair value, find the closest competitor to your region and use their salary range as a benchmark.

Your hiring budget

Getting a handle on what you can afford

One other major thing you will need to do before you jump into the hiring process is create a hiring budget. This budget includes not only what your company can afford in terms of salary and benefits, but any other expenses related to the hiring process, such as:

- Hiring a recruiting firm or headhunter (see page 20)

- Advertising the position in various media (see pages 48–54)

- Booths at job fairs or recruiting events (see page 60)

- Holding mealtime interviews or entertaining off site (see page 140)

- Flying in long-distance candidates for interviews (see page 142)

- Hiring a temp worker to support you while you are busy with the hiring process

- Giving a signing bonus as an added incentive to a top candidate

So how much should you plan to spend? That depends—on region, industry, type of job, and of course the recruiting methods you use. A recent survey conducted by the Society for Human Resources Management found that hiring costs vary widely by type of job—from $26,000 to $70,000 for an **exempt** (salaried) position, and up to $24,000 for a **nonexempt** one (a job with an hourly wage).

To figure out your own budget, the first thing you might want to do is find out if your company formally tracks cost-per-hire (known as CPH; see page 63). According to the Employment Management Association, CPH derived by dividing the total costs associated with recruiting by the number of full-time hires in a given period, usually a month. If the company does track CPH, you can find out what was spent on a similar hire in the past. If not, you'll need to sit down and assign a cost range to any of the costs you expect to have from the list above, and to any others you come up with.

ASK THE EXPERTS

I have a hiring budget of $90,000. I can spend up to $20,000 of this on hiring expenses other than salary. How might I break this down?

Again, this will really depend on your particular hiring situation, but a typical breakdown of a $20,000 hiring budget might look something like this:

Advertising, traditional: 20%	$ 4,000
Advertising, Internet: 5%	$ 1,000
Recruiting agency or temp help: 40%	$ 8,000
Employee referral program: 2%	$ 400
Job fairs/College recruiting: 5%	$ 1,000
Signing bonus: 15%	$ 3,000
Mealtime interviews: 3%	$ 600
Miscellaneous: 10%	$ 2,000
Total	$20,000

I'm not going to use a recruiter. Should I spend more on advertising?

Yes, if your budget allows. If you use a recruiter, you can expect advertising to account for about 20 percent of your hiring budget. If you don't, plan to spend about 70 percent on advertising, unless you opt to use mostly Internet ads, which cost less than traditional ones.

Our hiring budget is really tight. Where can I cut corners?

The most expensive item on a manager's budget is usually the headhunter or recruiting agency, so if you're on a tight budget, consider eliminating that in favor of hiring a temp worker to help you out so that you can devote more of your own time to the hiring process. If you do still want to use a recruiter, don't be tempted to hire the cheapest one, since you'll usually get the service you pay for. You can also save on hiring costs by putting more of your ad dollars into less expensive forms of advertising, such as online job boards.

Dealing with salary woes

What to do when you can't offer a competitive salary?

Once you have a clearer idea of the going rate for the position, revisit your hiring budget (see page 36). If you have allocated more than you'll need, lucky you! If the going rates surprised you, you're in good company. Most of us underestimate the cost of good help.

But think twice about cutting too deeply on salary. Offering competitive compensation packages are one of the chief ways companies win great talent. And ultimately you do get what you pay for. If you luck out with an overqualified candidate who is willing, for some reason, to work for less money, you risk having an employee who is resentful of the lower pay and will leave as soon as they get a better offer. If they leave a year later, it will cost you more in turnover expenses (see page 17) than the slight salary bump would now.

If you can't afford the going rate, know that for some applicants, certain benefits are as attractive as a higher salary, if not more so. A new employee who wants to get a degree, for example, may equate tuition reimbursement with a salary increase. Since you don't know which benefits will be prized by various candidates, find out about them in advance so that you can use them to hire someone who might otherwise demand a higher salary. Here are a few to check on:

- Matching 401(k) or other robust retirement program
- Family leave (including paternity) or sabbatical opportunities
- Domestic partner benefits
- Adoption reimbursement
- Tuition reimbursement
- Comprehensive medical benefits (dental, eye care)
- Sign-on bonus if hiring for a more senior position
- Stock options
- Flexible time or telecommuting opportunities

ASK THE EXPERTS

We've underbudgeted for an open position. Is there any way around this?

See if you can borrow from another line item on the company budget. But if the salary ceiling is firm, you have a few other options. One is to get creative and enhance some components of the pay package that don't really have a dollar value attached, such as more vacation time or better office space (see page 170 on compensation packages).

We need a full-time employee, but we can't pay the going rate. Now what?

Review the job qualifications you've put together and see whether you can do without any of them. You may also want to spend more time recruiting through job fairs at colleges and graduate schools to find younger talent. They'll lack experience, but if you're willing to put more into training, you may find a diamond in the rough. Another possibility is to hire a contingency employee; for more on that see chapter 12.

FIRST PERSON INSIGHTS
Unexpected benefits

"I had the tough task of hiring for a management position during a time when every department's budget had been cut and salaries were lower than usual. I found a wonderful candidate, but when I made him an offer, he told me that while he liked our company's mission, he'd been offered 10 percent more by a competitor. I explained that I couldn't offer more and ran down a list of benefits, hoping one would spark his interest. When I got to domestic partner benefits, his face lit up. He explained that his partner was a freelance graphic artist and the cost of his health care was more than the 10 percent salary difference we had discussed. Ultimately, that was the perk that made him choose us."

Amy M., Walnut Creek, CA

The job description

After you have figured out your salary range, the next step is to write a precise **job description**. Or, if you work for a larger organization or one with an HR department, there may already be a job description on file. Whether you need to write it from scratch or get it from HR, make sure you do get it—this document is essential to a successful hire, because it clarifies all the basic **job functions** (tasks) and requirements for the position. (See page 43 for a sample job description.)

In some cases, the job description will become the ad that you post to bring in applications. For example, it may be posted on your company's Web site or sent to HR so they can recruit internally. In other cases, you'll develop a shorter ad from the longer job description. This will immediately weed out some unqualified or inappropriate candidates.

The job description clarifies what you're looking for and helps you create a list of important job criteria (see page 44), which you'll use as a checklist as you go through the interview process. After you have hired someone to fill the job, the description also provides that new employee with a blueprint for the job and makes your expectations crystal clear from the beginning. And finally, it will serve as a handy tool every time you hire for this position in the future.

ASK THE EXPERTS

Is there any online information on how to write a job description?

Yes—what can't you find on the Internet these days? One good place to start is "How to Write a Job Description," a helpful and thorough article complete with samples, which you'll find on the Business Know-How Web site (**www.businessknowhow.com/manage/jobdesc.htm**). And a Web search for "how to write a job description" at **www.google.com** yields over 450 results! You can try the same technique at other search engines such as **www.altavista.com**, **www.yahoo.com**, and dozens of others.

WRITING A JOB DESCRIPTION

If you are hiring for a new position or there is no job description, there may still be corporate guidelines for writing job descriptions that you can rely on. If there are no guidelines, don't panic. It's simple once you understand the basics:

- Use clear, concise language. Keep sentence structure simple.

- Use nontechnical language whenever possible. The requirements and responsibilities of a job should be understandable even by a layperson.

- Begin each sentence with an active verb. Use present tense.

- Avoid gender-based language ("he" and "she"); instead, stick to neutral phrasing, such as "the candidate will."

- Qualify whenever possible the desired outcome of the job duties described, rather than just describing the methods for accomplishing that outcome.

A sample job description

Here are the various sections that go into most well-written job descriptions. Compare these to the sample at right.

Job title A two- or three-word title that would go on the employee's business card, or the term used to describe the position.

Job overview/objective Three or four sentences that briefly summarize how the position supports the company's objectives.

Responsibilities Include all the tasks the employee will perform. If you can, get an updated list of these from a previous employee and incorporate those. If you expect the position to develop, or you would like some flexibility, add, "Other duties as assigned by manager."

"Must have" skills These are the minimum skills the employee must have to perform the job successfully. Well-written skill descriptions usually begin with "the ability to." For example: "the ability to type 70 wpm," or "the ability to scan and optimize images using Photoshop."

Preferred skills The skills or special abilities that you would like candidates to have, but that a lack thereof would not disqualify them. For example, bilingual fluency for a medical office.

Requirements/qualifications Here you should indicate how many years of related experience or what kind of education or degree is required for the job. This also includes specific areas of knowledge and behavioral characteristics required (such as "the ability to interact effectively with customers").

Special requirements This covers any special requirements, such as a certain kind of driver's license or the ability to work overtime.

Reports to This is the person to whom the employee will report on a daily basis.

Salary If it is standard in your company to list salary, put a range or figure here. It is also common to write here, "Salary commensurate with experience."

JOB DESCRIPTION

Job title   Financial Analyst

Job overview/objective   Assess company's financial needs and strategies and perform various types of financial budgeting to increase company profitability.

Responsibilities   Must demonstrate a thorough understanding of corporate finance and a wide knowledge of capital markets. Must be able to communicate this information in writing and in conversation to audiences with varying levels of understanding.

"Must have" skills   BA in finance or business. Two years or more of related experience. Knowledge of financial software (Excel, Lotus, etc.).

Preferred skills   MBA. Two years or more of related experience at a Fortune 500 firm.

Requirements/qualifications   Ability to travel 25 percent of the year to branch offices nationwide.

Special requirements   Chartered Financial Analyst (CFA) designation

Reports to   Director of Financial Services

Salary   Commensurate with experience

The job criteria checklist

Keep it simple and focused

After you have written a job description or reviewed an existing one, it's time to create a job criteria checklist. This is simply a short list of the most important job criteria. You'll use this list later on to screen résumés (see page 68) and pick out potential hires.

Begin by reading the job description again, picking out the most important requirements that job candidates must fill. These can include specialized skills, educational background, employment history, training, test results (if applicable, they will come later; see page 76), and any other credentials or licenses required by the job.

Create a list of the top criteria, ordering them from most important to least important. See the sample at right for ideas. And remember to keep it simple—you'll be comparing this to résumés once you start receiving them, and chances are you'll have a lot of résumés to review. You can save the more detailed comparisons for later, when you're ready to start picking out candidates to interview.

JOB CRITERIA CHECKLIST

Position: Senior Support Technician

Required job skills and experience

- 3 yrs+ experience with network systems or database software

- BS degree in computer engineering or computer networking

- Current certifications as required by the department manager

- Evidence of successful project management and completion

- Knowledge of Spanish

Helpful resources

Tools you can use

BOOKS

Entrepreneur Magazine: Human Resources for Small Businesses
by William Sullivan

How to Compete in the War for Talent: A Guide to Hiring the Best
by Carol A. Hacker

High Performance Hiring
(revised edition, 2002)
by Robert W. Wendover

WEB SITES

The Salary Expert
www.salaryexpert.com
This handy site has free salary research info for hundreds of positions across the U.S. and Canada. Reports also contain explanations of how the cost-of-living in a particular region affects the actual value of the salary.

SalariesReview.com
www.salariesreview.com
At this site, you can purchase wage and salary reports and cost-of-living reports for thousands of cities across the U.S. and Canada, as well as for more than 200 other countries.

The Economic Research Institute
www.erieri.com
If you're really serious about salaries—or plan to hire for multiple positions—you can get a dynamic, robust tool for salary calculations at the Economic Research Institute. Its Salary Assessor® for Windows provides salary survey analysis in an easy to use software database that aids in the assessment of an organization's salaries and wage/salary competitiveness. ERI's salary survey data provides detailed median and mean salary-range information for over 4,756 positions in 298 U.S. and Canadian metro areas.

Home Fair
www.homefair.com
If you plan to advertise nationally and think you may need to relocate the employee, check out this site to get an idea of what the moving expenses will cost you if you offer to reimburse.

Absolute HR Solutions
www.absolutehrsolutions.com
Absolute HR Solutions offers a Job Description Writing Guide in MS Word that guides you through the process of writing job descriptions for any position and includes 22 sample descriptions to work from.

CHAPTER THREE

GETTING THE WORD OUT

Advertising the position

A job advertisement may be your first opportunity to communicate with prospective employees, so you want to make it good—good enough to get the city's most talented job seekers excited about the job even before they walk in the door for an interview.

Of course, communicating vitality and enthusiasm in only five or six lines of text can be a tall order. If you don't have the space to wow readers, at least make sure to include the most important elements, including how to contact you. Remember, clarity is of the essence. If job hunters like your ad but don't understand what the job is or whether their skills match the position, then it hasn't done the trick. Draw on the job description you wrote and produce a summary of the key parts of that document.

Here are some important guidelines:

- Be honest about what you want. While you don't want to be so specific that only three people in the world might qualify, you do want to state your expectations and requirements explicitly. If five years of experience are required, then say so, loud and clear.

- Use the ad to promote your company. If it has an excellent compensation package, for example, say it with an exclamation point. If you offer outstanding upward mobility, include that too. List as many of your perks as space allows, such as flexible hours, child care, bonus opportunities, and relocation reimbursement.

- Limit the use of abbreviations. While you can expect intelligent applicants to decipher a certain number of abbreviations fairly easily (e.g., "Exp a +" or "Refs req'd"), too many of them will make your ad incomprehensible. Don't forget: Keep it clear and simple.

THINGS TO CONSIDER

Location   Should you do a national or a local search? This will depend partly on the job skills and on your budget. For higher-level positions, you may want to draw candidates from across the country, so you may want to advertise in national papers. Or you may decide that online advertising, which has no geographic limits, is broad enough.

Time   How long do you want the ad to run? Ideally, it should be out there for as long as you will be accepting resumes. For example, if you need to hire within the next two months, run the ad for three to four weeks, or until the resume cut-off date.

Cost   Find out what different newspapers charge for advertising vs. online bulletin boards. Know ahead of time what percentage of your budget can be allocated to advertising (see page 36).

Reach and Target   How many people do you want to reach? Would a classified ad in daily newspaper with 1 million readers be more effective for this opening than an ad in a targeted industry newsletter with a circulation of 5,000? Likewise, would a highly trafficked, more general online job board be preferable to an industry-specific board?

Classified vs. select placement   Does it makes sense to run a more expensive, perhaps two- or full-color ad in, say, the jobs section of your local paper or in a trade magazine? Or will it serve your purposes to just run a simple line ad in the classifieds? Usually, lower-paying and lower-level jobs can be filled via less expensive classified ads.

Competition   Research the media you're considering to see if your competitors are advertising similar jobs. If so, before you place your ad, make sure it stacks up.

Design and text   Printing an attractive, legible ad is critical—for any kind of job opening. If you have a PR or communications department, ask for their help to design and write the ad. Or, if your budget allows, consider having an outside firm do it. In both cases, double- and triple-check for errors—you don't want to send the wrong message.

Elements of a good ad

What you can do to lure the ideal candidate

A good job ad does not need to be laid out exactly like the job description, but it should contain much of the same information.

Headline   This is the first thing job hunters will notice, so make it bold or extra large. You should advertise either the job title or the industry/business in the headline. In general, avoid overblown headlines like "Your Future Awaits You at BetterBiz Incorporated" or "Earn $10,000 per month!" Many people associate these with job scams.

Objective   Draw on your job description for this (see page 40). Condense the overall objective to one or two sentences max.

Skills/qualifications   Here, sum up the "must have" skills and the required experience or qualifications. If you can't fit it all in, make sure to include the absolute prerequisites for the job. Add one line on preferred skills, if space permits.

Benefits   Zero in on the key factors that attract new employees to your company. Is it the corporate culture? Location? The financial benefits? A great reputation? Advertise your most competitive benefits, such as a 401(k) program, profit sharing, or EOE (meaning you are an equal opportunity employer).

Salary   You can include your ceiling or your range offered. Or if you prefer to leave it open, you can simply say "highly competitive pay package" or "salary commensurate with experience."

Directions   Explain how you want résumés submitted and whether candidates can contact you by telephone (usually not a wise idea). Specify whether you want a cover letter (often a good idea for jobs that require good writing/communication skills) and whether salary requirements should be included.

TECHNICAL WRITER
Get A Jump On A Fast-Track Career

Are you a top-notch writer with a science background? Are you interested in the expanding field of biotech? You may be the new Tech Writer we are looking for. Communications department at successful biotech firm seeks writer with flawless skills and ability to understand scientific documents. BA or BS in science preferred, as well as journalism experience or prior tech writing experience. Quick promotion for high performers. Fax résumé and salary history to **writerjob@futuretech.com** by May 1.

ADMINISTRATIVE ASSISTANT
$11-13/Hour   FT/Days
Room to Grow

Award-winning fashion company located in downtown Philadelphia is searching for an Admin Asst. Beautiful offices overlooking the park. Must be detail-oriented with excellent communication skills and ability to work in a fast-paced environment. Prior exp. assisting high-level exec a must. MS Word & Excel skills req'd. Previous fashion experience a +. Huge growth opportunity! Highly competitive salary & benefits. E-mail résumé to **hr@hifashion.com** with subject: Admin. Pos.

Print ads

Finding a home for your ad

Once you have your ad polished and ready for prime time, it's time to hunt for suitable print venues to reach your preferred audience. First, make sure you know what your budget is for advertising (see page 52). Then allot yourself enough time to write the ad and to get it to the publication far enough in advance so that they will be able to print it on the dates(s) you've chosen.

Start with the classified sections of national newspapers serving your region. They'll likely have more expensive rates than the local papers, but they tend to be a first stop for job seekers and if you're not in there, you could miss top quality candidates. Spend a few extra dollars to get the bold headline or larger typeface or maybe even print your company's logo.

If you have a limited budget for print media advertising, pay attention to each paper's circulation, areas of greatest concentration, and demographics. Don't overlook the local angle. Advertising the job in college and university newspapers is an excellent way to recruit fresh young talent.

When working with a recruiter (see page 20), you'll want to go over the print advertising options that the recruiter suggests. You may be able to supplement the recruiter's strategy with placement ideas of your own.

Finally, consider placing an ad for the job in newspaper sections other than the classifieds, ones that might target your audience of potential applicants. If you're hiring for finance or other positions in business, buy ad space in the business section, since that's what already-employed people in that industry will be reading.

ASK THE EXPERTS

We're advertising the job on the Internet—do we still need to advertise in newspaper classifieds?

It is true that online recruiting has matured significantly over the past several years, but newspaper classifieds are still a major part of the job-seeking process. Most experts agree a combined effort—using two or more media to reach your audience—is best. Besides, unless you're interested in hiring only people under 30, you can't be positive they're plugged in to all the hottest e-recruiting channels. Bottom line: You have to go where the candidates are—and they're both online and off.

I'm hiring for a branch of our company in another city and am not familiar with the local papers there. How can I find out about them?

Most cities and populous or large counties have Web sites that provide tourism and commerce information, including a list of local papers. Call the local convention and visitors' bureau as well. And don't forget to ask your colleagues at that branch.

"HELP WANTED" STILL WORKS

If it's an assistant or retail salesperson you're after, don't be afraid to go back to basics and put that sign in the window of the store. There are big pluses to hiring from your customer pool; you gain an employee who is already somewhat knowledgeable about the product and probably likes the company, and is therefore more motivated to sell. Keep the ad simple though, and visible.

The Internet

Using the Internet as a recruiting tool

An Internet **job board** (a Web site with job listings) is the online answer to classifieds. Unlike newspapers, which many job seekers have to go out and buy, the openings on job boards are just a few mouse clicks away. They can be viewed 24 hours a day, and can be linked to your company Web site, an e-mail address, or an online application form.

While daily newspapers charge per day or week and by the size of the ad, online job boards usually charge a flat fee to run an ad for 30 days, or sometimes until the job is filled. This flat fee varies from about $25 to $75 per month for a basic posting; more for a boxed ad or homepage ad. Space is not a premium for basic postings on these sites, so you have more room to talk about the job and your company without having to pay extra. Résumés can be submitted to you via e-mail, which allows faster replies to your ad and can help cut down on paperwork. As part of the advertising package, some job boards also allow you to search their résumé database and contact qualified applicants. This could be an advantage if the site has a search tool that allows you to input keywords related to the position, which can turn up qualified applicants who listed those words in their résumés.

It's important to realize that as wonderful a tool as the Internet is, it can also eat up time in searches and digging through e-résumés. Given the number of boards out there, you'll want to do some research to find the right ones for your industry and job function. And make sure those you choose have a high hit rate (number of visitors per month).

Also consider how you want candidates to reply to your online ad. Specify whether you prefer to receive résumés in the text of an e-mail or as attachments —but be aware that certain kinds of attachments may be incompatible with your system. Realize that if you ask applicants to e-mail you directly, your inbox may be swamped. It's often better to use a separate e-mail address for this, such as "**hr@yourcompany.com**," or specify the listing by a job number: "**job25@yourcompany.com**."

POPULAR INTERNET JOB BOARDS

The online job market, which started with just four or five very general boards, exploded in the late '90s and now includes hundreds of sites—including highly specialized niche boards—where applicants can search for openings by **keyword** and post résumés for potential employers to find them. In 2001, 10 percent of job seekers found their new jobs online, according to a survey by Forrester Research in Cambridge, Mass. Monster.com tops the list in popularity, and Forrester expects it to dominate the U.S. online recruitment market by 2007. But before you go with Monster, check out the other industry leaders as well.

America's Job Bank (**www.jobsearch.org**)
Career Builder Network (**www.careerbuilder.com**)
Career Path (**www.careerpath.com**)
Dice (**www.dice.com**)
Job.com (**www.job.com**)
JobWeb (**www.jobweb.com**)
Monster (**www.monster.com**)
NationJob (**www.nationjob.com**)
Yahoo HotJobs (**hotjobs.yahoo.com**)

USING YOUR COMPANY'S WEB SITE AS A RECRUITING TOOL

Job boards aren't the only online recruiting option. Many companies now have a Careers section on their corporate Web sites—an inexpensive tool for attracting talent. They include info not only on specific jobs, but about the company and why it's a great place to work. Job seekers can search for jobs by keyword, job function, or location (if the company has several offices). If your company's Web site doesn't have a Careers or Jobs section, see if you can post the job in the About Us section.

Word of mouth

Use your own network to get leads

You never know where the ideal candidate might be found, and there's a good chance she could be a friend of a friend of a colleague. So make a list of the names of potential resources for your search. Include former managers and colleagues from previous employers. If you have relationships with your company's vendors or other business partners, plan to call them as well—though you should make it clear you're not trying to poach their people. Include friends on your list; they have jobs too. (And even if they don't, they know people who do.)

Take a methodical approach to reaching out to the appropriate industry organizations (and perhaps post internally there), to your university alumni association, and even to your church/synagogue or any volunteer organizations you might be involved in. Also, a trusted colleague on staff might have a contact for you—an industry pro, for example, who is qualified, eager, and available to work for you. Some career coaches estimate that 70 to 80 percent of jobs are secured by direct contact and networking or word of mouth.

If you belong to an e-mail list related to your own job, send out an e-mail letting the list know that you are hiring and what you are looking for. Recently laid-off employees often join e-mail newsgroups to network. You may not have met any of the people on an e-mail list, but the advertisement is free of charge.

ASK THE EXPERTS

We want to hire some bright young people. Where should we look?

One good way to start is to make an effort to develop relationships with a few professors at the local university. This can be an invaluable tool for your current hiring process and also down the road. Professors get to know dozens of students each year and can be a natural first resource when you're looking for qualified young go-getters.

Referral programs

Getting your work force to recruit for you

One of the best ways to identify and hire talented people, while lowering your **cost-per-hire** (see page 62) and motivating your existing workforce, is the **employee referral program**, or ERP. The ERP offers a cash bonus incentive—or less commonly, noncash awards like cars or vacations—to employees who refer people they know for jobs at the company, and who are then hired. So instead of having one headhunter working for you, you potentially have hundreds—or thousands, depending on the size of your company. And rather than spending $10,000 to $30,000 to recruit one person through a headhunter and other methods, you could spend as little as $250 for nonmanagement jobs. Bonuses for management positions are usually anywhere from $500 to $3,000, or a bit more for senior-level positions in finance or technology.

Some companies restrict the eligibility for a referral bonus to those jobs that are hard to fill, usually defined as any job that the company has already tried unsuccessfully to fill several times or for a period of weeks or months.

The bonuses are generally paid in two increments: half at the time of the hire and half when the employee has been at the company for six months or a year. Some companies will go further and enter those who've made successful referrals into a larger annual lottery for a special bonus prize.

Most ERPs are advertised on the corporate Web site, encouraging all employees to participate. Ideally, the amount of the bonus to be paid for each position filled should be listed with that job description to avoid any confusion.

ASK THE EXPERTS

Are there any statistics that show the effectiveness of ERPs?

There are surveys that attempt to measure effectiveness, at least by word of mouth. The Society for Human Resources Management, for example, recently conducted a survey of 586 HR professionals to find out how well their employee referral programs were going. Eighty percent said the programs were more cost-effective than hiring recruiting firms and 36 percent said ERPs were highly effective in increasing retention of current employees. The programs have been around for more than a decade and are now widely considered to be cost-effective and without much downside.

Doesn't an ERP encourage people to put as many people up for the job as possible to increase their chances of getting the bonus?

Not really. First of all, most employees are aware that the referral they make reflects on them; they don't want the company to hire someone on their recommendation who later turns out to be a problem. Second, most employees are going to be referring a close friend or relative. The job application and interview process is stressful and if the employee doesn't think the new candidate has a good shot at getting the job, they're not going to risk straining a relationship just to increase their chances of making a buck.

Campus and career fairs

Job fairs are an excellent way to reach qualified applicants, both newly graduated and more experienced. They take place on college campuses as well as in convention centers, hotels, and auditoriums. Typically organized like trade shows, **job fairs**, also known as career fairs, assemble dozens of employers in booths for a day, or sometimes two, and job seekers walk up and down the rows, "shopping" for jobs. To rent a booth, employers must pay a fee, which varies according to the size and location of the fair. But it can be worth it—your company can attract hundreds of applicants in a single day.

One big advantage of job fairs is that rather than just getting a faceless résumé to add to your stack, you get to meet applicants and spend a few minutes with them. Use the time to get a quick impression—as well as to find out who has the necessary skills. The booth is your first point of contact, so be sure to use attractive displays, materials, or demonstrations to highlight what is best about your company. Given that you are able to reach candidates en masse, career fairs are a particularly effective and economical option for companies looking to hire more than one person.

If years of experience isn't a prerequisite for the position you're filling, universities and colleges are fertile ground for finding fresh, eager talent. Many schools have robust on-campus recruiting and career development centers that are eager to develop relationships with local and national businesses. And many have **job books** or computer job banks in which you can list the opportunity if you are willing to submit the information in the required format. Others will allow you to post job descriptions on career bulletin boards, which can range from physical bulletin boards to a Careers section on their main Web site.

ASK THE EXPERTS

What are virtual job fairs?

Meant to be online simulations of traditional job fairs, **virtual fairs** link job seekers with employers via the Web. Some are really just Web sites that list job openings and allow applicants to send résumés by mail, similar to online job boards. But more advanced versions allow you to schedule real-time chat sessions with prospective candidates.

The career center of our local college won't allow us to hire interns unless they can receive class credit for their work. Why is this?

It may be the policy of that college. Some schools help place students in internships (part-time jobs paying a nominal wage) that don't earn them any college credit, but others require internships to have academic value. Some managers find the latter option too time-consuming, because they have to follow the school's guidelines for reporting on the student's progress, submitting grades, etc. But it can also be a great way to get motivated, intelligent talent for next to nothing.

BE PROACTIVE ABOUT DIVERSITY

Diversity recruiting (seeking out minority candidates) has become an important part of corporate hiring strategies, and one that many senior managers have started to demand. One way to reach members of America's minority groups is through diversity job fairs or expos, held around the country. Some are focused primarily on African, Asian, Hispanic, or Native American job seekers. Others cater to women, disabled people, gays and lesbians, and other groups that tend to be underrepresented in the workplace. The NAACP (**www.naacpcareerfair.com**) also holds diversity career fairs in cities nationwide all year long. Diversity Expo (**www.diversityexpo.com**) holds several as well. As with any other type of job fair, you will want to make sure that the focus is appropriate for companies in your industry.

The cost-per-hire concept

Making sure your hiring efforts pay ott

How do you measure which hiring process is the best and most cost-effective? For starters, you need to keep track of all your advertising tools. As soon as you place an ad in a newspaper or on the Internet or your internal job-posting site, start keeping track of the number of résumés you receive. If the classified you placed in a local paper isn't turning up good candidates after a couple of weeks, it's time to either reexamine your ad or pull it from the paper and find another vehicle.

If you are using recruiters (see pages 20–21), you need to keep track of the number of qualified résumés they are showing you. Make sure they're really going after candidates you can't get to without using them, rather than just relying on the same online recruiting tools you could be using for free. If the search is going slowly for legitimate reasons, use the time to get extra bits of wisdom by consulting with the recruiter on the salary.

Another way to track successful hiring methods is to ask qualified applicants to tell you how they heard about the job. You can include a checkbox on the application that asks how or where they heard about the job. Or if your company doesn't have application forms, ask in the pre-interview phone call.

ASK THE EXPERTS

Is there a way to measure our overall cost per hire?

Definitely—and this is well advised. One of the best-known and accepted staffing metrics is **cost-per-hire** (CpH), which is calculated by dividing the recruiting costs by the number of positions filled:

Recruiting Costs / Number of Positions = CpH

You'll have to determine what you consider recruiting costs and whether they include the salaries of anyone within the organization concentrated on staffing (including administrative staff). Once you start doing these calculations, you can compare your numbers to those of other companies using results of surveys like those from the Society for Human Resource Management (**www.shrm.org**) or benchmark reports like those put out by **www.staffing.org**.

Helpful resources

Tools you can use

BOOKS

WEDDLE's 2003 Recruiter's Guide to Employment Web Sites

Online Recruiting: How to Use the Internet to Find Your Best Hires
by Donna Graham

Employer's Guide to Recruiting on the Internet
by Ray Schreyer
and John McCarter

Recruiting on the Web
by Michael Foster

Headhunters Revealed!: Career Secrets for Choosing and Using Professional Recruiters
by Darrell W. Gurney

WEB SITES

Net-Temps
www.nettemps.com
This online job board specializes in temporary, contract, and temp-to-hire jobs.

Nicheboards.com
www.nicheboards.com
Offers access to specialized job boards in fields such as sales/marketing,

finance/accounting, IT, retail management, and call centers.

My Safari Jobs
www.mysafarijobs.net
A niche-industry job board that links to jobs in accounting, pharmaceuticals, education, finance, engineering, legal, and sales, among others.

The New York Times Job Market
www.nytimes.com/pages/jobs
This excellent resource for employers includes a monthly Job Market Confidence Index and weekly updates on industry trends and workplace issues.

Diversity Job Fairs
www.diversityjobfairs.com
Offers a list of diversity job fairs in cities around the country.

Referral-Trak
www.referralmarketing.com
This company sells software that lets you put your ERP online in a private company database. Employee Referral Marketing, Des Moines, IA, 50325 (515) 221-1733.

SCREENING APPLICATIONS

Getting organized

Establishing a screening system

Get organized before résumés, cover letters, applications, or other materials come in. Set up a file folder system; you'll need one folder for each résumé. Into this folder goes the résumé, cover letter, any supporting materials, and any notes you'll take about the résumé (see page 68), or notes you'll take later on any phone conversations (see page 72), or on the interview itself. Never write directly on the résumé itself, in case it needs to be reviewed by another manager or your boss.

On the outside of the folder, mark the date you received the application. You can file the folders chronologically too if you wish. (There's no guarantee that early submitters will necessarily be your ideal candidates, but it's always good to know which applicants were most eager to apply and were particularly organized and punctual.)

Make sure to impose a strict deadline or cutoff date for résumé and application submissions. Depending on how urgent the hiring need is, you might give yourself anywhere from one week to four weeks to collect résumés. After the deadline, create a folder for backup résumés, in which you'll place any additional ones that come in. These will be useful in the event that none of the earlier submissions work out and you need a fresh pool of candidates, or if you find yourself needing to hire for a similar position.

BLOCKING OUT TIME

One of the best time-management techniques is simply blocking out time. Since the tasks associated with reviewing résumés are not necessarily of a fixed length, it's easy to let them seep into the rest of your day. Therefore, impose time on them. Block out an hour or two each day, or more if it's necessary and you have it to spare, for reviewing new résumés and making prescreening calls, and that's it for that day. When résumés are delivered to your inbox throughout the course of the day, simply put them in your résumé folder and forget about them until the time you set aside for them. Carefully delineating when you'll be working on that job search and when you won't will go a long way toward helping you maintain a level of efficiency.

Résumé screening

Reading between the lines

Although résumés can cover the spectrum when it comes to length, font, and color of paper, when you get right down to it, they all supply more or less the same information, namely, skills, job experience, and educational accomplishments. As the résumés start to pour in, make sure to keep a copy of the most important job criteria in front of you (see page 44), and pay attention to the following:

Overall appearance Is the résumé legible? Easy to follow? Are there obvious spelling or grammatical mistakes? Even if the position isn't for a proofreader or copy editor, sloppiness or carelessness are bad signs. And with spell-checking available, there's no excuse for bad spelling.

Minimum requirements Quickly screen the résumé for critical skills or anything that, if absent, would disqualify the applicant. If you're looking for someone with at least three years' experience in corporate communications, you can rule out anyone with less than that. Likewise, if someone has several years' experience but lacks a degree in marketing, a prerequisite for the position, there's no reason to compromise.

Alignment of experience Check how closely the candidate's previous work experience aligns itself with the job criteria you are trying to fill. Screen for similar job titles and functions. How recent was the last relevant job?

Key verbs Screen for relevant terms, such as "managed," "initiated" or "supervised," particularly for a leadership or managerial position.

From this preliminary screening, you should be able to set aside several "maybe" candidates to follow up on, as well as a few "definites." The next step is to compare their qualifications in more detail by weighting the job criteria and seeing how well the applicants stack up (see page 70).

ASK THE EXPERTS

One candidate has many years of relevant job experience but seemed to take a career detour in the middle of it. Is this a red flag?

Not necessarily. In the past, managers who hired focused almost exclusively on linear career paths, and those who ventured outside the lines were considered less dependable or less focused. But the '90s changed that thinking, thanks to the birth of an entrepreneurial culture that led many in the work force to detour at least temporarily to follow their dot-com dreams. If you think the employee is otherwise qualified, it's certainly worth asking in an interview to explain the detour and how it might have added to, rather than subtracted from, his or her suitability for the job.

WHAT THE COVER LETTER CAN TELL YOU

Cover letters, while not nearly as important as the résumé, should still be considered carefully. A cover letter is the candidate's first opportunity to impress you, and one that communicates enthusiasm, originality, and a basic understanding of the job, your industry, and/or your company is the sign of a motivated candidate. Check that the applicant has paid attention to the needs of the position and has made an effort to match up his experience—this is much better than vague phrases about skills. The cover letter should also be formatted professionally and addressed either to you or to the contact listed in the classified ad.

Weighting skills

Assigning more importance to the most critical skills

As you start to come across résumés of candidates that look like potential good hires, you need some system for evaluating how well they fit your job criteria. Simply checking off which candidates have which skills is useful, but scoring them on those skills is even better. That's why it helps to figure out which skills are more critical to the job than others and to weight them accordingly.

Say, for example, you are hiring a senior support technician person for your department, and you've already identified five key job criteria: 1) 3+ years experience with network systems and databases; 2) BS degree in computer engineering or computer networking; 3) Current certifications as required by the department; 4) evidence of successful project management; 5) knowledge of Spanish.

If you judged each criterion equally, you would end up choosing to interview the candidates who have the highest total scores. But what if, for your purposes, a total lack of experience with network systems and databases would disqualify the candidate, even if he or she qualified in every other category? Weighting the criteria gives you a chance to allow for that.

Here's how you do it. Go back to your original list of job criteria (see page 44), and use them to create a table like the one at right. 1) Assign each criterion a value from 1 to 5, with 5 being very important. 2) Rate from 1 to 5 how well each candidate meets each criterion, with 5 being the highest score possible. 3) For each candidate, multiply the score for each criterion by the value assigned. 4) Now add up all the points for each candidate; the result is that candidate's weighted rating.

The chart on page 71 demonstrates how with a weighted approach you would rate candidates for the tech support job, and puts the most emphasis on the importance of having networking experience.

EVALUATING CANDIDATES
BY CRITERIA

First, weigh the criteria List the required skills and expertise from your job description and assign a point value from 1-5, with 5 being very important.

Criteria	Rating
3+ yrs experience with network systems and database software	5
BS degree in computer engineering or computer networking	4
Current certifications as required by the department	3
Evidence of successful project management and completion	2
Knowledge of Spanish	1

Next, weigh the candidates Create a table like the one below, listing the top criteria and their weight in the far left column, as in this example for the tech support job. As you review the best résumés from your pile, write the name of the candidate at the top of a column and rate from 1-5 how well the candidate fits the criteria. Leave blank if they do not fill the requirement. Then multiply each rating by the weight assigned to the criterion, and write this number in the next column—these are the scores you will then add up to see which candidates fit the most important job criteria best. Place an asterisk (*) next to the name of applicants to be interviewed. In this case, Jenna and Alan's higher scores—especially for the top criteria, network experience—make them good candidates for interviewing.

Key Criteria / Weight	Brandon's rating	Brandon's weighted rating	Jenna's rating	Jenna's weighted rating*	Alan's rating	Alan's weighted rating*
3+ yrs network exp. /5	-	-	4	20	5	25
BS computer degree /4	5	20	5	20	4	16
Certification /3	5	15	2	6	5	15
Project management /2	3	6	3	6	4	8
Spanish /1	3	3	4	4	2	2
Total Score		44		56		66

Phone interviews

You've checked through all the résumés you've received and have discarded the obviously unqualified applicants. There are 12 viable candidates. What now? Consider phone interviews. While in-person interviews can take anywhere from 30 to 90 minutes, a telephone interview doesn't need to last longer than 15 minutes for you to get what you need to move on to the next level.

The telephone interview is usually used to check whether a candidate meets the job requirements. It's easy to fudge a few items on the résumé or leave out some vital piece of information. Some candidates just hope to get in the door, figuring they can sell themselves once inside. The phone call allows you to address any vaguely worded job descriptions that may have crept into the résumé. If you're not clear on what "supervisor of large projects" means, this is a good time to ask. Clarify any other ambiguous phrases, too, such as "participated in" or "assisted with."

Also double-check that the candidate has the key criteria you need. Have a list of them—education level, management experience, software skills, training—handy when you place the call. If you can, prescreen at least your top 10 candidates and another 10 or so maybes.

You can't assume a candidate has a degree just because a college is listed, so if that level of education is a prerequisite, confirm a graduation date during the phone call. Fill in any missing dates or résumé gaps and confirm the availability of references.

If you're sure you want to see the candidate at the end of the prescreening call, feel free to arrange a time and date, but if not, simply thank the candidate for the information and the time and say you'll get back to him or her within the next day or two.

ASK THE EXPERTS

I tried doing a telephone prescreen and wound up in a 45-minute conversation with the candidate. At that rate, wouldn't I be better off just bringing them in for interviews?

Yes—at that rate. It can be difficult, when you're trying to be polite and friendly and make a good impression to stick to the business of the phone call. Be polite, yes, but be direct and focused and stay in control. Don't ask any open-ended questions. Act as though you're simply filling in blanks on a test and this candidate has the answers. Go down your list, and when you have each item answered to your satisfaction, end the call.

Job applications

A way to get more uniform data

Just a few decades ago, a **job application** was the standard way to apply for a job. Then along came the résumé, which more or less took the place of job applications as the key screening tool for hiring. Naturally, job applicants prefer résumés, which allow them to highlight their best features and to put their qualifications in the best possible light in order to sell themselves.

But job applications aren't entirely obsolete. They are still used for all sorts of jobs, from entry level to senior positions. One advantage is that they're structured and uniform, which makes it easier for you to skim to the most important sections. You're also more likely to get accurate information on job applications simply because candidates have to answer very specific questions and then sign their names at the bottom to attest to their correctness.

Some companies use applications as a second-level screening tool. In this scenario, applicants submit résumés and then the employer contacts those who have made the first cut and sends them a job application to fill out prior to coming in for an interview. This way, employers get some of the benefits of free-form submission, but they don't let candidates get out of answering some of the more pointed questions. Toward that end, you should make sure your application is customized as much as possible to your needs.

ASK THE EXPERTS

What is a "weighted" application form?

On a weighted job application, a certain value is assigned by the manager to each of the items on the form, allowing you to effectively sort candidates based on their education and experience (see pages 68–69 for information on how to do this). Of course, this requires you to have predetermined (or at least have a pretty good idea of) which criteria will predict superior job performance. If you don't already have a weighted application, it's worth developing one only if you hire often for similar positions, because it does take time and consideration.

KEEPING IT LEGAL

In a job application, do not include questions related to the following :

- Race
- Religion
- Gender or sexual orientation
- Age
- Ancestry or national origin
- Marital status
- Handicaps or disabilities
- Arrest record
- Military service
- Height or weight, unless directly related to the position
- Political affiliation or membership in any political or social organizations

Do include questions that will give you information regarding:

- Name, address, and other vital stats
- Educational background
- Employment history
- Additional skills/experience

Pre-employment testing

To test or not to test? Depending on the job, tests are sometimes the only way to ascertain if the candidate has the skills you need.

Skills or proficiency tests, for example, are used to objectively assess a candidate's ability to perform basic job-related tasks. If typing a certain number of words per minute is critical to the job of an administrative assistant, then a typing test would be a legitimate screening tool. The same is true for tests that measure knowledge of word processing or software. More customized tests, such as a proofreading exam or an architectural drafting test, would also be appropriate. It is critical that any such test measure only those skills the employee must have to perform the job properly.

Psychological and personality tests are another matter. They are designed to reveal characteristics such as assertiveness, ability to cooperate, stability, and psychological health—things that might not come out during an interview. But some assert that these assess test-taking abilities rather than job skills. And many of the once-accepted questions on personality tests have been successfully challenged in court for invading candidates' privacy.

Integrity or honesty tests also walk a fine line. Smart managers use them only when they can be legitimately defended as having a direct relationship to the nature of the job, such as handling cash, guarding property, or working with controlled substances, like pharmaceuticals.

Before deciding which tests, if any, to administer, consult HR and, if necessary, your corporate legal department. And before using any test, search for scientific backup substantiating the accuracy of that test; you can often get this via the supplier or company that developed it.

ASK THE EXPERTS

Are personality and psychological tests useful for high-level positions?

They are indeed used for executive-level jobs, and some argue that these sorts of tests protect the company by ensuring that a psychologically unstable manager doesn't go on to endanger other employees. But even advocates of these kinds of tests admit their results are highly subjective and need to be weighed in conjunction with employment history, interview impressions, and reference checks.

A WORD ABOUT DRUG TESTING

Substance abuse can be a huge corporate liability, costing time and money. So it's not surprising that many corporations want to test candidates for illicit drug use. But keep in mind that the laws on drug testing vary by state. Some allow testing only for public safety, others only for positions related to driving, still others allow testing for any position and others don't allow them, period. Because the laws over drug testing are constantly in flux, make sure to check with your state department even if you think you knew what the rules are. If it is legal, you need to decide when to administer the test. Some companies test after the offer has been made, while others use it as a screening tool. In either case, make sure you give notice to the candidate that you intend to test for drugs.

Helpful resources

Tools you can use

BOOKS

Staffing Organizations
by Herbert Gerhard
and G. Heneman

*Hiring and Keeping
the Best People*
by the Harvard Business
School Press

*Smart Hiring: The Complete
Guide to Finding and Hiring
the Best Employees*
by Robert W. Wendover

*101 Hiring Mistakes Employers
Make and How to Avoid Them*
by Richard Fein

WEB SITES

Tapestry.Net
www.tapestry.net
This company offers a variety of applicant
screening services, in customizable packages, based on artificial-intelligence technology.

PeopleBonus
**www.peoplebonus.com/PB/Small
BizRésuméScreening.html**
Offering résumé screening services for both
large and small companies, PeopleBonus
uses the so-called predictive matching
technology to score and rank all incoming
résumés based on how well they match the
job description.

AssessmentCompany.com
www.assessmentcompany.com
This company, in partnership with Profiles
International, offers a host of online assessment and testing solutions for business and
individuals.

Pre-Employment Drug Screening
**www.employmentdrugtesting
.com**
This company provides drug testing for
small and medium-size businesses.

Mind Tools
**www.mindtools.com/pages/main/
newMN_HTE.htm**
This site offers a plethora of techniques
for managing time and projects more
effectively.

CHAPTER FIVE

PREPARING FOR THE INTERVIEW

Doing résumé research

So you've picked out a handful of candidates you want to talk to in person. What's next? Going straight to the interview? Not just yet. Before you do that, maximize your time and effectiveness by doing a little background research based on the résumé.

First, take a closer look at the companies each person has worked for. If you don't recognize them by name, do an Internet search and find out how big they are, what they do, and who they partner with. This will give you a rough idea of the sort of corporate culture the candidate is used to.

Next, check the résumé for any projects the candidate says he spearheaded or contributed to. If you are hiring a Webmaster, for example, you should be able to view a Web site or two created by the applicant. If a candidate interviewing for an advertising account-manager position claims to have created winning campaigns at XYZ company, go to that company's Web site and search for the relevant materials. Your enhanced knowledge of the candidate's accomplishments will help you make the most of the time you have—and it will immediately impress the interviewee.

As you delve deeper into a candidate's résumé, make additional notes in your file about anything on the résumé you have questions about (remember—not on the résumé itself but on a sheet of paper in his file). Be on the alert for creatively concealed gaps in employment, puffed-up descriptions of minor jobs, and suspiciously overpadded accomplishments. In the interview, plan to ask about these and job titles or responsibilities you are not familiar with—basically, anything that is new to you.

ASK THE EXPERTS

I searched online, but I wasn't able to find anything about one woman who is a strong candidate for our graphic designer position. Now what?

If you weren't able to locate a Web site or supporting materials to look at, and you know you would like to see them before you schedule the interview, call the candidate or send her an e-mail asking for links to work that she's done, or ask her to bring in samples or a portfolio if you decide to interview her. The same would go for a job that requires writing; ask the candidate to bring in writing samples. A candidate who is interested in the position will be eager to help you out.

DOING BACKGROUND RESEARCH ONLINE

To find out more about a candidate, assuming there is information available, try searching for the name using one of the major search engines—such as **www.yahoo.com**, **www.google.com**, or **www.altavista.com**. Type the full name, first and last, exactly as it is spelled on the résumé, in quotes, in the search box:

"Sally Wright"

That will tell the search engine to find any instance of those two names only as you've typed them, rather than any other configuration. Obviously, if the name is common, you'll wind up with thousands of useless leads. Try adding information to the quotes that would help find what you're looking for:

"Sally Wright" "marketing assistant"

To find the companies listed on the candidate's résumé, you can try typing the company name into the address box at the top of your Web browser, adding ".com" to the end, or you can look for the company Web site via a search engine, putting the name in quotes. If you still can't find it, try using Hoovers Online at **www.hoovers.com**. For more on background checks, see page 161.

Early reference checks

Confirm the stated facts

You may be thinking, "What—reference-checking so soon? I haven't even met the candidate yet!" Many managers leave all their reference checking for the end of the hiring process, almost as a formality before making the offer. But, unfortunately, some applicants have a tendency to embellish their résumés—or even make things up. By doing a bit of early research, you can whittle down the list of people to just those who are genuinely qualified.

Since most applicants do not attach a list of references to their résumés, you won't be able to do a complete check. That's okay. What you can check at this stage are facts related to educational degrees and honors, as well as any professional memberships. These are just a quick phone call away. Not all of the details on a résumé are critical to the position, but since it is important to hire honest employees, checking their forthrightness is a good move.

If you want to dig a little deeper, you can call the HR manager at past companies, up to, but not including, the current company, just to verify that the candidate worked at each when he or she claims. In general, the more you can check up front, the less you'll have to verify later when you'll likely be a little pressured to fill the spot.

ASK THE EXPERTS

Can I call the candidate's current employer to verify employment?

Not unless the candidate explicitly agrees to that. And then, you can do that only after you make a job offer. Most people understandably don't want to broadcast to their current employer that a job search is under way. There are cases where a layoff or reorganization is imminent and a candidate will have his or her boss's help in securing a new position. But if you haven't gotten the express green light and you call a current employer, you could open yourself up to a lawsuit if the candidate experiences any negative repercussions from that call.

FIRST PERSON INSIGHTS
Check now, save time later

"A few years ago, I was hiring someone for our sales department. The position required at least a B.A. in marketing and two years' experience selling in our industry, which we specified in the ad. After going through résumés, I chose eight candidates I really liked, all with the right qualifications—and then some. Figuring the new hire would come from one of those eight, I sent the rest to HR for future hires. I interviewed all eight and got the race down to two outstanding candidates. I was planning to have them meet a few senior managers in the department and then discuss compensation. But first, I decided to sit down and call their colleges. I found out that one candidate, though he had job experience, had completed only a year of college, and the other candidate had not earned a double degree with high honors, as he had stated. I had to start back at square one. Since then I always check basic educational requirements up front. That way I don't waste my time."

Karen B., Miami Beach, FL

Why prepare?

Chances are, if you've hired before, you've said to yourself, "I don't need to write out a whole list of questions. I'm good on the fly. I'll ask the candidate to tell me about herself and then I'll just ask questions based on the information she gives me."

You might want to reconsider that strategy. The interview is not a casual conversation; it is a focused question-and-answer dialogue. That's why it's a good idea to prepare a list of key questions that every candidate should answer. This will give you a basis for comparing the responses once the interview process is completed. Naturally, you'll also want to ask impromptu follow-up questions specific to each candidate, but if, at least, the fundamental questions are the same or similar, you can compare and contrast and decide more easily which candidates were most impressive. Being prepared also makes you look that much more professional.

The interview is also your prospective employee's first encounter with you and with the company. Since the ideal candidate may have more than one job offer, you want to impress her as much as she probably wants to impress you. If you're prepared and well organized, that will challenge her to step up her professional tempo to match yours.

FIVE TIME-HONORED QUESTIONS

Even with the best of intentions, it does happen: Time gets away from you and you find you have an interview scheduled for that day, but have had little time to prepare. Or you may be called into an interview by another manager without having a chance to review the applicant's résumé. In these situations, there are a few fail-safe questions that will help you get the interview started:

1. *"Why are you leaving your current position?"*

This will give you much-needed insight into what would not be a comfortable environment for this candidate. If your environment is similar, take note. If, however, the candidate is currently unemployed, ask why, what happened at the last job, and what he has been doing since then.

2. *"Can you take me through your previous work experience and tell me how you think it prepares you for this position?"*

This should tell you whether the candidate has experience that is directly relevant, as well as whether this position would be the next logical step for the candidate.

3. *"What are you looking for in your next position? How does it fit with your long-term career aspirations?"*

You'll hopefully hear why the candidate is there and whether he is highly motivated to make a move. Understanding where the job fits into his long-term plan will give you an idea of how committed he'll be to the job and the company.

4. *"What are your greatest assets?"* or *"Why do I want you on my team?"*

This gets right to the point of why you should hire her by asking the candidate to sell you on herself. From this, you can get an idea of the applicant's confidence level and her own perception of her skills.

5. *"Can you tell me about yourself?"*

This oldie but goodie serves a dual purpose. As an icebreaker, it gets the candidates talking and gives you an opportunity to gauge their communication skills and their ability to summarize key points quickly. You get an idea of initial chemistry, and you should get some openings for follow-up questions. Watch out for rambling monologues, and be prepared to reign it in if the answer goes on too long.

Behavior-based questions

Predict future success by drawing on a candidate's past experiences

If you ask a candidate what he would do if an irate customer called him, chances are his answer is going to be part fantasy—what he likes to imagine he would do, or what he thinks you'd like to hear him say. What you need to know is what he is most likely to do given his past experience. This is based on the premise that past behavior is a better predictor of future behavior than candidates' responses to hypothetical future situations.

Enter **behavior-based questions**. The idea is that when you ask for descriptions of situations or challenges that have already come to pass, the answers you get are far more candid, realistic, and telling. You go beyond the hypothetical to the real stuff. And it's a lot harder for the candidate to invent details when he already has a true past scenario in his head.

Behavior-based questions focus on specific skills, knowledge, and the ability to perform particular functions of the job. How did the candidate make decisions or form judgments? How did he analyze problems and resolve them? How did he communicate with others? Questions in a behavioral interview usually begin with "Tell me about a time when . . ." or "Describe a situation where . . ." There are variations, such as: "This position requires excellent organizational skills, the ability to multitask, and the ability to lead a team on various projects. How does this relate to what you were most recently doing?"

10 GREAT BEHAVIOR-BASED INTERVIEW QUESTIONS

1. *"Describe a situation where you had a conflict with someone and how you handled it."*
This is an opportunity to see some depth of character and get a sense of how well this person would fit in with your team. If the candidate says she can't recall a time when she ever had a conflict, that's a red flag.

2. *"Tell me about a time when you increased productivity or improved operations."*
Find out how the candidate contributed to the bottom line. Make a note to check this information with references.

3. *"What is the one thing you would want to improve at your current/former company and how would you do it?"*
This gives you insight into the candidate's strategic thinking, as well as perhaps more information about why he is leaving.

4. *"Tell me about a time when you gave exceptional customer service."*

5. *"Describe a time when you had to juggle several tasks at one time and how you prioritized your work."*
When it comes to interviews, one could argue there's no such thing as getting too specific. It may take a candidate a moment to come up with a particular scenario, but if she can't, then you know juggling wasn't a big part of the job.

6. *"Give me an example of a situation where you had to exert leadership to get a task done or problem resolved."*

7. *"Tell me about a time when you adapted your personal style to work effectively with people who were different from you."*

8. *"What are the skills you still need to acquire in order to advance your career?"*

9. *"Of all the people you've ever worked for, who did you enjoy working for the most and why? Who did you enjoy working for the least and why?"*

10. *"What is the most useful criticism you've ever received?"*

Personality-based questions

Giving classic queries a makeover

Aside from experience and skills, you also need to know if a potential hire might be a good fit. To measure that, you need to ask a few questions that reveal a candidate's personality. To add a little freshness to the interview, try taking a new approach to these classic workhorses:

"What are your greatest weaknesses?"

Asking a candidate to evaluate weaknesses can sometimes invite a rehearsed answer that may not reveal anything. What you may get is something like, "My greatest weakness is that I'm a workaholic" or "I take on too much responsibility." No candidate will be eager to brag about his shortcomings. Instead, try asking: "On your most recent evaluation, what areas needed improvement? Was that a fair assessment?" or "In which areas would your most respected critic say you need improvement?"

"How do others describe you?"

This, too, may invite self-promotion—"People say I'm hard-working and honest"—that won't reveal anything about the candidate's proficiency in any particular competency. Ask the candidate for specific situations in which she has demonstrated the qualities she mentions.

"Sell me a pen."

It's not a bad idea to ask a candidate for a sales position to sell you something in the interview, but try to stay away from the overused "Sell me a pen." Chances are, the candidate has sold pens to 10 other employers and has perfected his sales strategy. But unless your company actually sells pens, all you'll have found out is that he knows how to prepare for an interview. Another option is to ask the candidate to play headhunter, selling himself to you. Add a behavioral question: "What was the most difficult sale you ever had to close? Why? How did you accomplish this? "

"Where do you see yourself in five years?"

Nine out of 10 interviewers love to ask this one, but, in all likelihood, a much lower percentage actually get anything useful out of it. The candidate will be hesitant to answer honestly for fear it will count against him—particularly if he hopes to have your title in five years. Instead, try asking, "What are your long- and short-term career goals?" Or: "If anything were possible, which position in this business would you aspire to have?"

A WORD ABOUT THE STRESS INTERVIEW

The classic **stress interview**, in which a candidate is faced with a mostly hostile interview situation, complete with long, uncomfortable pauses and an argumentative or confrontational interviewer, has long since been discredited as unnecessary. Most interviews are stressful enough as it is, and unless you are interviewing someone for a position in the Pentagon, your new employee will probably not have to face such a hostile environment. Clearly, if the job is senior level, in sales, or in a category that requires the ability to handle significant pressure, then you do want to see whether the candidate can handle the heat on an interview. Just keep in mind that the candidate doesn't need to handle any more pressure in the interview than he or she would on the job.

The legal ABCs

If you're like most managers, when you set out to hire, you'd much rather focus on getting the best person for the job than on hiring laws.

On the bright side, however, the great thing about hiring laws is that in addition to protecting potential hires and current employees, they help ensure that you and your company get the best person for the job, because you will be hiring that person based solely on experience rather than superficial or irrelevant criteria that can sometimes cloud one's judgment.

Hiring laws are based on rulings by the **EEOC**, or the Equal Employment Opportunity Commission (**www.eeoc.org**). It was established in 1965 to promote equal opportunity and keep employers from discriminating against potential employees. It's the same commission that would contact your company if any employees or would-be employees made a complaint.

There are a number of federal EEO statutes to be aware of that could impact your hiring practices. In addition to the list at right, some states, cities, and counties also prohibit discrimination on the basis of sexual orientation; others, such as San Francisco, go even further and won't do business with companies that don't have similar antidiscrimination laws on the books. Be sure you're aware of your own state's and city's rules before you begin the hiring process.

HIRING LAWS

These are the five important federal laws
you need to know about when you hire; they are
designed to protect applicants and employers from
discrimination.

1. Title VII of the Civil Rights Act (1964)

This statute makes it illegal to make hiring, compensation, promotion,
or firing decisions based on race, color, national origin, gender, or religious
practices and beliefs. The Civil Rights Act of 1991 upped the ante for
employers by allowing applicants to seek compensatory and punitive dam-
ages for acts of discrimination.

2. The Age Discrimination in Employment Act (1967)

This act prohibits you from making any hiring or promotion decisions
based on how old an individual is.

3. The Pregnancy Discrimination Act (1978)

This amendment to Title VII makes it illegal to treat any applicant or
employee differently because of pregnancy or related medical conditions.

4. Immigration Reform and Control Act (1990)

This act establishes penalties for employers who knowingly hire illegal
aliens. This one is tricky, because you cannot ask questions about race or
national origin that might put you in violation of Title VII. But you can
ask all applicants whether, if hired, they will have proof of citizenship.

5. Americans with Disabilities Act (ADA) (1990)

This act prohibits discrimination against qualified individuals with a
disability. It covers both physical impairments, including physiological
disorders and cosmetic disfigurement, as well as mental impairments,
including psychological disorders, mental retardation, and some learning
disabilities that substantially limit major life activities, such as seeing,
hearing, walking, and caring for oneself. (For more on accommodating an
applicant with a disability, see page 114.)

In addition to the laws listed above, some states, cities, and counties
also prohibit discrimination on the basis of sexual orientation.

Putting it into practice

Following your company's EEO policy

Before you do any interviewing or hiring, you'll want to familiarize yourself with your own company's policies and procedures. The EEOC lists a number of requirements for employers who want to "assert defenses" (make a valid, defensible argument) against discrimination or sexual-harassment claims. These requirements include posting notices regarding discrimination laws and conducting periodic training.

Not all laws and statutes apply to all companies. For example, the Age Discrimination in Employment Act (see page 91) applies to companies with 20 or more employees who work 20 weeks or more per year, while Title VII (the Civil Rights Act; see page 91) applies to employers with 15 or more employees. Larger companies, typically with 100 or more employees, are required to file an annual form, known as the Employer Information Report EEO-1, which communicates to the EEOC the demographics of the company's workforce.

If you are not in HR, you don't need to be on top of every legal detail, but it is in your best interest to investigate your company's policies and to learn how to comply with various EEOC requirements. This way, you'll be adequately protected and informed in the event that an issue arises with the EEOC.

Get a copy of the most recent employee handbook and read it carefully, then be sure to follow all the standards set by your company. If there are things you are unclear on, sit down with the head of HR or arrange a phone conversation and ask all the relevant questions.

ASK THE EXPERTS

Do I need to have an employment law expert check my hiring process?

It is highly recommended that you have a legal expert look at your selection process and job criteria, as well as any screening tools you plan to use, such as pre-employment personality, skills, or drug tests. Chances are, if you work for a large company, your HR department has a contractual relationship with a law firm that handles all that, or your company may have legal counsel on staff. If you've introduced any new documentation, make sure HR knows about it so it can be reviewed by the appropriate experts. The law can be tricky and it changes often, so it pays to be cautious and cross all your t's.

What is a "bona fide occupational qualification"?

This is the exception to any discrimination rule. It means that if you can prove that criteria that appear to be discriminatory are a must for the job, your practices may not be found in violation. For example, the religious beliefs of a member of the clergy being hired for a specific religious organization are usually considered a **bona fide occupational qualification**. But be careful about including such a qualification in a job posting, because it can be very difficult to prove in a court of law.

THE AT-WILL RELATIONSHIP

Unless your company's policy is to have the new hire sign an employment contract, you and he will have **at-will relationship**, which means you and the company may terminate the employment relationship with the employee at any time at your discretion. Find out if your company's handbook includes a form, to be signed by the employee and returned to you or to HR, acknowledging at-will employment status. If that is not included in the handbook, get a form from HR to include either in the job application or in the offer of employment.

The candidate's questions

The best time to cast your company in a positive light

Preparing to answer candidates' questions about your company is
one of the easier things to do in advance. Have a list of bullet points
about the company and the position with you at every interview. By the
time you get through two or three interviews, you probably won't need
it anymore, but have it in your stack just in case.

Note: Before you go into your answer, ask the candidate what he
knows about the company. By doing that you'll find out whether he's
done any homework in advance, which shows a certain degree of moti-
vation and initiative. You'll also know where to start your intro.

Expect the candidate to have some knowledge of the position. But
knowing the title and a few basics won't really give her a sense of what
her day-to-day tasks would be. It's often helpful to go through a day
or two, explaining what would be expected of her. Then discuss how
her performance will be evaluated and what she can expect in terms
of promotions or bonuses. Using the interview as a kind of mini-pre-
orientation will also make the new hire's first days that much easier. As
you do this, prompt the candidate for a reaction: "So how does that
sound to you?"

This is also your opportunity to sell the candidate on the company,
particularly if you're really interested in her. Expand on the kinds of
things that you have highlighted in your ad, including special benefits
or perks like casual Fridays or a subsidized cafeteria. If you are a small
company without many perks, emphasize the intimate environment and
the opportunity she will have to learn in-depth about various aspects of
the business.

BE READY TO ANSWER
THESE QUESTIONS

- "Could you give me examples of what my day-to-day functions would be?"

- "What does it take to be successful in this position?"

- "How does this position fit within the department and the organization?"

- "What special projects or functions would I be involved in or responsible for?"

- "What would a positive evaluation about me say?"

- "Assuming I do well, what kind of advancement can I expect? How soon and to what position?"

- "What is the company's financial position?" Be ready with figures. Savvy candidates will want to know that they are moving to a financially sound company that, barring unforeseen circumstances, is poised to grow in the coming months and years.

THE TRUTH—AND NOTHING BUT

When it comes to hiring, what you say during interviews and job offers has legal weight, meaning that any statements you make can be treated as a binding contract if a legal question arises. If, for example, the candidate says that, as part of the experience he is seeking, he would like to head up a new product development group, and that's not part of the immediate scope of the job, don't imply that it is just because you want him to work at your company. If you do, and later you have to let him go for whatever reason, he can sue you on the grounds that you thwarted his career objectives. The best advice: Stick to the truth.

Helpful resources

Tools you can use

BOOKS

*96 Great Interview Questions
to Ask Before You Hire*
by Paul Falcone

*The Manager's Book of
Questions: 751 Great Interview
Questions for Hiring the Best
Person*
by John Kador

*267 Proven
Interview Questions*
by Mel Kleinman

*How to Become a
Skillful Interviewer*
by Randi Toler Sachs

*Strategic Interviewing:
How to Hire Good People*
by Richard R. Camp,
Jack L. Simonetti,
and Mary Vielhaber

WEB SITES

Power Hiring
**http://behavioralinterviewing.
powerhiring.com**
Offers a host of information about the
behavioral-interviewing technique, as well
as on performance-based interviewing, an
alternative touted by the parent company,
Power Hiring, Inc.

Kathy Pennell & Associates
**www.pennellseminars.com/
behavioral_interviewing_
seminar.htm**
Consulting firm that offers behavioral-
interviewing training seminars.

SkillSoft
www.skillsoft.com
This e-learning company offers courses in
developing effective interview questions,
with a focus on behavioral interviewing.

CHAPTER SIX

THE INTERVIEW

Managing your schedule

Balancing your regular workload with a candidate search

As you've probably realized after prescreening résumés, hiring can become something of a part-time job. As you head into the interview phase, you'll need to manage the process so that it doesn't get away from you and eat up all your time.

Try to schedule several interviews back to back in a single block in the morning or afternoon. That will be less disruptive than having them spread throughout your day, which can impede your progress on other important work projects. Some managers schedule all of their interviews over a three-day period or a week. That can interfere with getting work done on other projects, but some find it helpful to get all the interviews out of the way in one shot. Just be careful: After 5 or 10 candidates back to back, you can start to lose focus and you might be unable to remember much about each candidate, which is why note-taking (see page 105) is such an excellent idea.

The best times for interviews are either mid to late morning, after your first tasks of the day are done (and you've finished your first cup of coffee!), or early to mid afternoon, after lunch but before you start thinking about winding down your day.

USING A CALENDAR

Unless you have several dedicated assistants, it can be tough to keep track of all those interview appointments. So if you didn't have a planner before, or your planner consisted of a handful of stickies matted together, making a new hire is the perfect excuse to start keeping track of your time in an organized way. If you go the paper-based route, you'll want an organizer with a calendar that has day slots large enough to list each of your appointments clearly. Day Runner Inc. (**www.dayrunner.com**) and Franklin Covey (**www.franklincovey.com**) both make organizers in all shapes, sizes, and colors. Choose one that allows you to see the full week's appointments, so you'll know whether you've scheduled too many interviews for that week or can slot in a few more. Palm makes a handy desktop tool (**www.palm.com**) that you can **sync** with a **handheld personal digital assistant** (PDA) for organization on the go, and Microsoft Outlook is a good desktop program too.

Showtime!

Be relaxed, friendly, and on time

As your very first in-person meeting, the interview is the first opportunity for both you and the candidate to form initial impressions. Since every applicant who steps into your office could potentially be The One, it's important to put your best foot forward each time.

Make sure to give yourself adequate time to focus mentally before the interview, ideally clearing your schedule five minutes ahead of the meeting time so you can skim the résumé again. Also, by scheduling in prep time, you'll avoid being late to an interview and giving the candidate the impression that things are always "a little crazy around here."

Choose a reasonably quiet and comfortable location, one where you won't be interrupted. Some managers prefer to do their interviewing on neutral ground, such as in a conference room or in a quiet café, or off-site, where potential coworkers will not know about it. If you conduct the interview in your office or cubicle, forward your phone to voice mail or ask the receptionist to hold your calls. A call at the wrong time can disrupt the flow and cause you to miss important information. Most candidates feel more comfortable with a desk or table separating them from you, so try to avoid sitting next to the person at a long table.

If possible, greet candidates yourself in the waiting area, rather than having them ushered into your office. This makes it slightly less formal. If you can't do this, rise to greet candidates when they arrive—and smile.

ASK THE EXPERTS

Is it necessary to offer refreshments at every interview?

No, it's not required. However, your goal here is to put the candidate at ease as much as possible and to get him talking. One way to do that is by focusing on common courtesies such as offering a glass of water or a cup of coffee, or offering to hang up his coat. How the candidate responds to these common courtesies can tell you a lot about how comfortable he is with polite social interaction and basic etiquette.

How important is the way the candidate is dressed?

That depends on your company and your own personal style. But even if your company's dress code is relaxed, you should expect candidates to "dress to impress." After all, they don't know the dress code before they're hired, so unless the position clearly doesn't warrant it, they should be erring on the side of formality if they're really interested. If everything else about the candidate is great, but your office requires a certain level of dress and the candidate is wearing sneakers, pose the question directly: "We wear business attire here. Would you be willing to work in a suit every day?"

IS LATENESS FORGIVABLE?

The old school insisted that lateness, for any reason, was unacceptable. But we all know that accidents will happen and unexpected delays can throw even the most conscientious of us off course. The real question is, how did the candidate handle it? Did he call to let you know he was running 15 minutes behind schedule? If calling wasn't an option, did he greet you with an apology and a reasonable explanation? You don't need people prostrating themselves, but accountability and responsibility are highly important qualities. If the candidate respects your time and feelings, there's a better chance he'll behave similarly with clients and other colleagues.

Body language

Take note of nonverbal cues

The first five minutes of an interview can easily set the tone. As you go about breaking the ice with the candidate, perhaps by asking if he had any trouble finding your office or how his day is going so far, start paying to attention to his body language.

Why? Simply put, you can learn a lot from a candidate's body language. Is he or she relaxed, yet attentive? Making eye contact? Smiling when appropriate? How is he sitting? A candidate who is slumped in his seat during the interview could be lacking in confidence, not overly concerned about making a good impression, or simply have bad posture. If the candidate sits with his arms folded tightly across the chest or in a hunched, defensive position, this would seem to contradict his statement that he's "very good with people."

Be aware of your own body language as well. Fiddling with things on your desk, tapping your fingers, looking out the window repeatedly, and checking your watch are all signs of impatience and disinterest. Be an active listener (see page 104), nodding encouragingly where appropriate and keeping an open expression on your face. Don't interrupt and don't let silences drag on too long. Be friendly and direct.

BODY LANGUAGE IS NOT UNIVERSAL

When you are evaluating the candidate's behavior, keep in mind that behaviors considered appropriate in one culture may be considered inappropriate or even offensive in another. Making direct eye contact, for example, is considered respectful and a sign of honesty in American corporate culture, whereas in some Eastern cultures, this might be overly familiar or rude. Since these differences can be hard to interpret, if you see behavior that truly seems out of place, don't jump to conclusions; remind yourself that it may be a result of cultural difference.

NONVERBAL CUES TO NOTICE

During the interview, take note of the following types of **nonverbal cues**. Positive cues usually mean the applicant is excited about the position and trying to put her best foot forward, while a preponderance of negative cues can mean she is hiding something or is not really interested in the job.

Positive Cues	Negative Cues
Interested expression	Blank expression
Some facial animation	Avoidance of eye contact
Good eye contact	Rapid eye blinking
Audible, steady voice	Mumbling, low voice
Clear enunciation	Rapid speaking
Energetic, upbeat tone	Monotone
Erect posture	Slouching or lounging
Both feet on floor	Bouncing leg or foot
Hands resting in lap	Playing with objects
Some slow gestures	Overly rapid gestures

Listening skills

Listening closely to the answers will allow you to probe for more

Hiring experts advise spending roughly 80 percent of the interview listening and only 20 percent talking. That can be harder to do than it sounds; some feel that talking more puts them in a more managerial light. Others have difficulty handling silences, so they talk to fill them when they should be asking other questions to elicit more information.

Attentive listening is one of the most important skills an interviewer can have. Asking good questions is only part of the equation; you stand to learn much more from what a candidate actually says, so pay careful attention to her answers.

Listening well will give you the opportunity to ask the right follow-up questions and to probe for more detail. If the candidate mentions casually that she's living here in Denver now but that she grew up in Seattle, where all her family and friends are, it would be a good idea to ask a few questions about whether she's happy living here and whether she has any plans to return to her hometown any time soon.

Listen to your own responses too: They can encourage enthusiasm, or discourage candidness if a candidate catches on that you don't approve of a particular attitude or behavior. If a candidate mentions that her last job involved occasional long hours, follow up with: "How did you feel about working long hours?" rather than "You don't have a problem working long hours, do you?" Alternatively, try asking: "How many hours a week do you think it would take to get this job done?"

Take the time to review a candidate's answer and fill in any missing information. If you don't understand something, ask for clarification. If you ask for more details and the candidate gives you the same answer but in different words, don't let it go. Make sure you close the interview with the information you need.

ASK THE EXPERTS

Should I be taking notes during the interview? And won't that interfere with my ability to listen?

Unless you have a superhuman memory, taking notes is really the only way to recall the details of a particular interview. The question is whether to take notes during or right after the interview. One solution is to leave a blank space after each question on your list. Jot down the bare minimum you need to remember a particular fact about the candidate. Then, immediately after the interview, while the answers are still fresh, write down as much as you can remember about your impressions and what the candidate said—being careful not to write anything that could be construed as discriminatory, like disparaging race- or age-related comments. Always play it safe, even in your notes.

FIRST PERSON INSIGHTS
The ripple effect

"Last year I had to replace someone in our company's accounting department. We were a bit confused about what we were looking for, and in the end, the person we hired wasn't a good match. During his training period, other employees ended up shouldering more work to compensate for his shortcomings. One in particular was so disgruntled that she began looking for another job. She had been a star player for eight years but just couldn't handle another rocky transition period with an underperformer. As manager, I wasn't even aware of how much extra backup she'd been providing. Fortunately, she told me before making the decision to leave, and I was able to tell her that the new hire was leaving for a more suitable job. But this experience taught me a valuable lesson about the ripple effect of bad hiring."

Dara F., Austin, TX

Interview myths

It's not all in the handshake

A number of myths related to interviewing have developed over time. They can interfere with successful candidate selection, so it's a good idea to be aware of them. Here are just a few:

Myth 1: **"I should be able to tell in the first five minutes whether I'm going to hire this person."** It usually takes 5 to 10 minutes for candidates to settle in and get over their nerves, so avoid making snap judgments. You may find out halfway into the conversation that the person you'd written off has exactly the experience you need. So allow the interview to progress naturally and see what unfolds.

Myth 2: **"It's all in the handshake."** Sure you'd like to get a handshake that's firm without leaving a mark. But there are cultural differences, as well as personal differences, that result in different kinds of handshakes. If it really bothers you, keep an eye out during the interview for other evidence supporting your first impression.

Myth 3: **"The best candidate will clearly 'shine' and stand out from the rest."** That would be nice, but it doesn't happen all that often. In fact, if one candidate is so head-and-shoulders above the rest of the pool, you should probably make sure his salary expectations are aligned with what you can offer. Most likely, you'll need to do some prodding and quizzing to find the diamonds. Also, don't assume that the candidate will necessarily volunteer all the great accomplishments that might lead you to pick him. Many top-flight candidates get nervous and forget; they need your probing questions to remind them.

Myth 4: "I should evaluate candidates against each other." There is a natural temptation to stack candidates up against each other and pick whoever comes out clearly above the rest. But what you should really do is evaluate them against your own criteria and standards, which you should make a list of before you start to interview (see page 42). For one thing, this will help prevent you from ending up with the best of a so-so bunch. For another, comparing and contrasting could lead you to mentally discount a highly qualified candidate in the middle of the interview because she didn't laugh as hard as the other candidate did when you made your standard opening joke.

Myth 5: "It's the candidate's task to decide whether this job is the best career move for them. All I can do is present the facts." You could leave that task up to the candidate, but if this job isn't the best career move for the candidate, he will eventually figure that out and may seek a different job soon after starting. As manager, you need to play part interviewer and part career counselor. By understanding whether this job represents the next logical move in a candidate's career path, you will know whether: the candidate will be happy in the position, and how long he is likely to stick around. If it sounds like he is overqualified or is taking a step down—possibly because he was recently laid off— you may end up losing that person six months down the road, when he gets a better offer. If he is currently employed, ask why he is leaving and what his next position would be if he didn't leave. Doing this will also help you cut down on the likelihood of a counteroffer by a current employer.

Off-limits topics

The things you are not allowed to ask during an interview are out-lined in the rulings of the Equal Opportunity Employment Commission (EEOC; see page 90) and cover everything from race and disability to age and marital status. Yet being overly cautious with your questions can undermine your ability to ask probing questions and be thorough. But fear not; having a good understanding up front of what you are and are not allowed to ask in an interview will not only keep you out of legal hot water, but will make it easier to have a constructive interview. Here are a few questions to steer clear of:

"How old are you?" This is the most direct form of the question and just asking it can give an applicant ample fodder for an age discrimina-tion suit if the person is over 40, or looks older, even if your reasons for not hiring that person had nothing to do with age. Other variations that raise a red flag: "When were you born?" "When did you graduate high school?" "In how many years do you think you'll retire?"

"Are you married?" Questions related to marital status are off-limits, so don't ask for a maiden name and refrain from asking where the can-didate's spouse works. Nor can you ask whether he or she has children. All you can do is explain the requirements of the job and ask whether the candidate would be available to put in the hours.

"Where were you born?" It might be a nice icebreaker, but as far as the law is concerned, it's a no-no, transgressing the rules concerning national origin, birthplace, and citizenship. Likewise, you can't ask whether a candidate is a U.S. citizen, although you may ask applicants if they can produce proof of U.S. citizenship if offered the job. Other problematic twists are, "You have an interesting accent—what is your first language?" and "That's an unusual name—is it Spanish?" These could be called out as discrimination based on national origin.

ASK THE EXPERTS

What if a job requires working on Saturday? Don't I need to find out if the applicant observes the Jewish Sabbath?

No. You only need to find out if the applicant can work on Saturdays, which is what you should ask, without referencing religious affiliation or observance.

What if the interviewee volunteers information about religion or marital status?

That's fine—just don't ask follow-up questions or say anything that would make you appear overly interested in that information. Even if it isn't related to your decision not to hire a candidate, he could still make a case that it was.

OTHER QUESTIONS TO AVOID

- Are you a citizen of any other country?
- What is your medical history?
- What is your religious affiliation?
- Would your religion prevent you from working on weekends?
- What holidays do you celebrate?
- What is your sexual orientation?
- Are you H.I.V. positive? Do you have AIDS?
- Have you ever filed for worker's comp?
- Do you have a disability?
- Do you have a history of substance or alcohol abuse?
- Have you ever been arrested?
- Have you ever declared bankruptcy?
- What kind of discharge did you receive from the military?

Handling their questions

The interview process is a two-way street: Not only are you interviewing a candidate, but she is interviewing you and the organization to see whether it really is a good match. So, before an interview, be prepared for questions the candidate may ask, and make sure to prepare a short introduction about your organization (see page 94). Honest answers will help ensure the best fit between the candidate and the job.

Here are some examples of questions you might be asked:

What is it like to work here?
- How long do people work here, and why do they leave?
- How do employees talk with senior management?

What will my job responsibilities look like?
- What are the major tasks of this job?
- What expectations do you have for the position?

What support will I have in meeting job requirements?
- What kind of budget is there for projects, and who determines it?
- What kind of administrative support is there?

What kind of authority will I have?
- Who will report to me? Who will be my supervisor?
- What decisions will I be able to make alone? With approval?

How will my performance be evaluated?
- How often can I expect to have a performance review? When is the next one? What system is used? Who will do it?
- If I do well, how might I be rewarded?

"RED FLAG" ANSWERS

Candidates may ask the following questions about your company, and if they do, phrase your response carefully. Certain answers may be viewed as a sign of underlying instability in your company, which may make them decide to pass up a job offer from you.

"Is there an open-door policy here?"

"Red flag" answer: "We have a standard procedure for submitting queries to senior staff or requesting meetings." This vague answer may give the impression that you are trying to hide some organizational problem.

Better answer: "Sure we have an open-door policy." Or, "Our company tends to be a bit more formal, but you can always schedule a meeting with managers if you need to." An honest, straightforward response.

"Who had this position before, and why did he leave?"

"Red flag" answer: "That is confidential," "It's not really important." This gives the impression that you're hiding something about the last employee, and that maybe he resigned or was fired under duress. This could lead the candidate to believe this position is dead-end or problematic, with unclear duties or an extreme workload.

Better answer: "He is pursuing another opportunity elsewhere." Probably true, and spares the candidate any distracting and possibly misleading details about the last employee.

"Can you describe the coworkers for this position? What is their experience and length of time working here?"

"Red flag" answer: "I haven't had time to learn who's in the department." This could lead the applicant to think that people are so overworked in your company that no one knows each other. Or that you don't know anyone in this department because there is a lot of turnover at your company—neither is something you want to brag about.

Better answer: "We recently hired a lot of new people and I'm still learning their names." This gives the impression that this is a dynamic, growing company where the manager takes an active interest in meeting all new employees.

The panel interview

The **panel** or **group interview**, in which the candidate sits around a table with three or more interviewers who each have their own questions, brings a number of strategic benefits to the hiring process.

For one thing, it saves time, assuming candidates would have had to meet with each of those interviewers separately. Candidates won't have to give the same answer over and over again (nor will they be able to rehearse answers in the process) and they won't have to hang around all day being shuttled from one office to the next.

Second, if the job is technical or contains multiple functions, it helps to bring people with varied expertise to the table so that all functions of the job can be covered in the same interview. It will also give the candidate a clearer picture of what the position will entail.

The panel interview also tends to be more revealing. One interviewer will ask a basic question, another will follow up with a more probing question, asking the candidate to clarify, and a third interviewer may be taking notes on the answers and devising another follow-up. The interplay often inspires more creative lines of questioning.

Also, keep in mind that not all good managers are good interviewers, so with the panel interview, weaker interviewers can fall back on those with better questions. Finally, having three or four people present at the same meeting tends to eliminate personal biases and ups the chances of making a successful hire, since you're likely to have some agreement on the choice.

For the best results, be sure all people present have read the job description and have received a copy of the candidate's résumé in advance. Interviewers should not interrupt one another or argue in front of the candidate. The goal is to maintain an organized front and to get the required information in the most efficient way possible.

ASK THE EXPERTS

How many people should be on a panel interview?

That depends on how many people you think have the skills and experience necessary to conduct the interview. In general, panels tend to have three to five people, with more people sitting on technical panel interviews. Having too many interviewers can turn the interview into a roundtable, and you may hear more from current employees than the candidate. If you do decide to do a panel interview, make sure the candidate knows about it ahead of time. It is generally more stressful than a one-on-one interview, and it will help her to be prepared if she is informed ahead of time.

What is role-playing in a panel interview?

In this take on the "good cop, bad cop" routine, two interviewers will divide questions between them, with one asking the friendlier questions and the other taking a more aggressive role. The advantage of this is that having at least one ally in the room can make the candidate feel more at ease, while he will still have to answer tough questions.

A disabled candidate

The legal protocol for considering candidates with disabilities

Great, you have a candidate who is perfect for the job. But since she uses a wheelchair, you are naturally concerned about how she will go about doing the job. What do you do?

The Americans with Disabilities Act (ADA) requires you to make "reasonable accommodations" for the physical or mental limitations of an otherwise qualified applicant or employee who happens to have a disability. It's good to be fully aware of ADA laws before you start the hiring process, since accessibility issues can pop up anywhere along the way. There are, for example, rules regarding the accessibility of the job application; a blind person may need an application read to them. Your HR department can help you stay on top of these laws.

Often, a candidate will tell you up front what he needs. But just in case, be sure the interview space is wheelchair accessible. Check for handicap parking spaces, ramps or step-free entrances, accessible rest-rooms, and elevators if the interview is not on the first floor.

Asking disability-related questions during the interview can be tricky, and some are strictly prohibited (see list at right). If you plan to ask any candidate about accommodations, the best way to do it is to make it an across-the-board question—one you ask every candidate on the tele-phone, *even before* the interview is scheduled. You might try, "Is there any special accommodation that you'll need for this interview?"

Feel free to discuss a disability with the applicant in the interview if he brings up the topic or makes a request at that time. The EEOC rec-ommends asking the disabled applicant for potential solutions, since he will be better versed in what has worked in the past. In some cases, this could save the company money, since a disabled person may suggest a lower cost solution than you might have thought of on your own. The one exception to an employer's obligation to make reasonable accom-modations is if this would place "undue burden" on the business (i.e., prevent the business from operating).

Though it's not necessarily a legal issue, maintain appropriate etiquette around a candidate with an obvious disability. Avoid staring at any impairment, for example. In general, maintaining a friendly, warm disposition will put the candidate at ease while making it clear to all that you, as the manager, have no issues with disabilities.

ASK THE EXPERTS

What about emotional or mental impairments?

There are a number of emotional and psychological impairments that qualify people for protection under the ADA, including workers with anxiety disorders, depression, schizophrenia, and bipolar disorder. A mental impairment is included if it limits "a major life activity" (such as dressing or feeding oneself) or if the applicant or worker has a record of such an impairment or is known to have the disability. The impairment must be long term and documented.

Which questions can't I ask about disabilities?

- Have you ever been treated for mental health problems?
- Are you disabled?
- How did the disability happen?
- What is the prognosis?
- Do you have a disability that would interfere with your ability to perform the job?
- How many days were you sick last year?
- Do you have high blood pressure?
- How much alcohol do you drink each day or week? Have you ever been treated for alcoholism? (Alcoholism and past drug addiction can be a protected disability; current use of unlawful drugs is not protected.)
- What medications are you currently taking?

Common mistakes

Now that you're actually doing it, here are a few sand traps to avoid as you go through the interview process:

■ **Using the interview to quiz on the résumé** Too often, managers waste time confirming information they already have in front of them, usually because they haven't made a thorough list of questions. Instead, use the résumé as a way to get into a deeper discussion about past work experience and then move on to details that aren't on there. If you really want to double-check the info, do it with references.

■ **Spending too little time with the candidate** Some managers feel they can get a good handle on a candidate in 15 minutes or less. And for some jobs that don't require much expertise, that may be true. But for most others, the bare minimum you'll need is a half hour, and for jobs with more responsibility, an hour. Remember, some candidates will need a good 10 minutes just to warm up and get comfortable. If you leave too little time for discussion, you will miss key points that should go into your decision-making process. If you only have half an hour or less to spare for each candidate in the first round, plan to bring people you like back for a second round.

■ **Revealing too much** Your company probably has its quirks, politics, and bureaucratic headaches—as does every company. You, having worked there some time, probably know a great deal about the company and you may feel an obligation to air all of the potential problems up front so that you won't be accused of misleading anyone. But telling the candidate that your boss "likes to micromanage" or that you think the company's mission statement is not followed rigorously probably isn't the best way to bring in top talent. Even if you have issues with the company, let the applicant reach his own conclusions.

ASK THE EXPERTS

When I interviewed one candidate, I wrote "accent too heavy, and image is not hip enough for us" in my notes, and my supervisor blew up at me when I passed him the file. Why?

It's a common mistake for interviewers to write down their subjective perceptions of a job candidate, but this can land your company in legal hot water if a candidate ever suspects that your rejection of him was based on his ethnic or religious background, height, weight, or a host of other personal characteristics (see pages 108–109). Always be careful to document only any shortcomings related to an individual's lack of talent, abilities, or experience—and stay away from making negative notes about your personal impressions. For example, it would be fine to write of one candidate, "Had difficulty remembering responsibilities at last few jobs. Not dressed appropriately for interview— might not be good for front-desk position." A statement such as, "Age-related memory loss may be a problem, plus really overweight and badly dressed" could lead to some legal headaches.

AVOID THE HARD SELL

The line between selling your company to the candidate (which you have to do a bit of) and overselling is admittedly a fine one, but it's a good thing to be aware of. Some managers will inadvertently go off on a sales pitch and before they realize it, they've spent 30 minutes cheerleading for their company. This can turn out to be a real Achilles' heel, particularly for entrepreneurs who are excited about the company and are used to selling it to investors and new customers. Remember that you're not trying to get seed money out of your job candidates, so hold off on the hard sell. And note: If they weren't interested in the company and the job, they would not be there in the first place. Keep your pitch to 10 minutes, if you can, and spend the rest of the time on them.

Helpful resources

Tools you can use

BOOKS

How to Become a Skillful Interviewer
by Randi Toler Sachs

Strategic Interviewing: How to Hire Good People
by Richard R. Camp,
Jack L. Simonetti,
and Mary Vielhaber

The 250 Job Interview Questions You'll Most Likely Be Asked . . . and the Answers That Will Get You Hired!
by Peter Veruki

WEB SITES

Peak Search
http://virtual2.pcisys.net/p/ peaksearch.net/hiringtips.htm
Offers hiring tips for employers.

Interview Strategies
www.Interviewstrategies.com
Designed to help candidates get ready, this site also offers useful information for managers as well.

Body Language
www.lichaamstaal.com/english
An in-depth exploration of body language as a communication tool.

CHAPTER SEVEN

INTERVIEWEE TYPES

The chatterbox

Keeping the talkative candidate on track

Though no two job candidates are the same, it's likely that as you gain more experience in hiring, certain interviewee "types" will start to emerge. One of these is the "chatterbox." Knowing how to handle this type of interviewee and others can make the interview process run a lot more smoothly.

First, the chatterbox. Here's a common scenario: You start off the interview with a little pleasant small talk about the weather. Ten minutes later, you've gotten the complete rundown on how he coped with yesterday's sudden downpour, but haven't managed to squeeze in one job-related question.

There are some people who don't need any encouragement to talk. Just mention a topic and they're off and running. But it's critical that you reign them in. Otherwise, the interview is just a one-sided conversation. It's often those managers who go into an interview unprepared who will let a candidate go on and on, grateful that he is filling the awkward silences. They will encourage the candidate to continue even after the question has been answered because they're not sure what to ask next.

The best tools for dealing with a chatterbox are a prepared list of questions and a willingness to interrupt a monologue. Once you feel you've gotten the gist of an answer and want to move on, try letting the candidate know through a subtle shift in position or by nodding and then looking down at your question sheet.

If you really feel the interview getting away from you, or it's getting a bit too casual, pause for a moment and say, "I'm really enjoying our conversation, but I do have a few questions left that I have to ask you, so why don't we switch to those now?" That will signal to the candidate that you'd like to inject a little formality, and he should heed the cue.

ASK THE EXPERTS

I don't want to hire a time-waster. Shouldn't I rule out an overly talkative candidate?

Not necessarily. It's true, there are candidates who figure that if they can keep the banter going or entertain you with a few dazzling stories, you may not notice that they don't have the experience or the skills you are looking for and that you'll choose them for their charm. But before you write off a talkative candidate, try to find out what's behind the candidate's verbosity. Use questions to probe the facts. You may find she is very qualified but gets nervous when put on the spot.

The aggressive interviewee

When confidence gets out of hand

This candidate marches in like he owns the place. He greets you with a very firm handshake and the familiarity of an old friend. He sits down, leans way back in his chair, and crosses his legs widely. Before you've asked your first question he's well into his first monologue, highlighting one of his many accomplishments. You feel like you should be impressed, but you can't help feeling a little uneasy with the way he keeps finishing your sentences.

Because overconfidence is one way candidates cope with feeling nervous and insecure—in addition to being overly chatty—you don't necessarily have to rule out this candidate immediately; there are, after all, career counselors and headhunters who mistakenly advise job seekers to act like they already have the job. Career coaches may advise candidates to ask a probing question that may not be appropriate or may sound presumptuous.

Also keep in mind that what you're seeing could be a snapshot of what you'll end up with full-time, and an aggressive employee may not respect authority or be much of a team player. To learn more, ask specific questions that explore how the candidate handles authority. For example: "Tell me about a time when you disagreed with your boss and you were right. How did you handle it?" Whether he was actually right is irrelevant (and you can't know unless you plan to call the former boss). But you can tell a lot about attitude from the response. Also consider asking, "What do you feel you learned from your former (or current) manager?" If the candidate openly speaks with disrespect about a former employer, it could be a sign of trouble. And direct at least a few questions to the issue of team play. Ask for an example of a situation where the candidate helped the team solve a problem or reach a specific goal. If he can only come up with examples of individual stardom, you may want to think twice about taking this candidate to the next level in the hiring process.

ASK THE EXPERTS

Isn't it true that sometimes the best producers are brimming with confidence? What if my team needs a star player or two?

That's your judgment call. But it can be hard to keep people working as a team when they're competing to produce. Conventional wisdom says that people who cooperate can get more done than one or two star players who produce but also undercut the efforts of a team.

THE CANDIDATE MAY BE OVERLY ARROGANT WHEN . . .

■ Your questions don't get answered. When you ask probing questions or want to drill down in a particular area, you get answers that don't really respond to the questions. You may get a long-winded response that sounds chock-full of information but actually contains very little substance other than a healthy dose of industry jargon.

■ You keep getting interrupted. Beware of the candidate who talks over you or tries to finish your sentences, as well as gets impatient or hostile when asked probing but necessary interview questions. Neither behaviors are great traits to display during a first interview.

■ The candidate challenges you. If you ask a question and hear, "I'm not sure that's relevant to this position," don't take it lightly. Likewise, be warned if you ask about an acronym on a résumé and get back, "I'm surprised you don't know that one!" Some candidates think they can get the job by showing they know more than their prospective employer, who will think, "Wow! I need that guy on my team!" But remember, there's a reason that you're on that side of the desk.

■ The interview feels like it's not in your control. The aggressive interviewee will try to control the interview by talking about things he feels confident about, rather than what you want to talk about.

The nervous candidate

Consider this scenario. The candidate arrives and you try to make small talk about her drive over or the lousy weather; she responds by laughing a little too loudly and nervously. You need a hankie after you shake her hand because her palms are so sweaty. She then proceeds to knock over a trash can on her way over to your desk and sits down, red-faced and obviously uncomfortable.

Before you make any snap judgments, remind yourself that many people do get very nervous at the beginning of an interview, but once they warm up and become comfortable, they do just fine. So make some small talk and allow adequate time for the candidate to settle down. Start with some general comments about sports or the weather you've been having lately. You may want to keep this interview a bit less formal than you would for someone less anxious. And you might want to address the issue directly. Tell the candidate that formal interviews can make anyone a little nervous. Smile and encourage her to take a deep breath and relax—you're not out to get anyone.

If the nervousness continues, then you'll have to decide how to weigh that. If you're filling a high-profile, stressful position in the company or a job in sales that will involve a lot of cold-calling or networking, you do need someone who can maintain composure when meeting new people or when challenged. But for other kinds of positions—data entry clerk or another nonmanagement job that doesn't require frequent customer meetings, for example—it may not be a deal-breaker if everything else looks good.

It can be tempting when interviewing someone who is obviously uncomfortable to ask yes-or-no questions or to "rescue" the candidate by interrupting him or her. But keep in mind that doing that won't help you or the candidate in the long run, because you probably won't hire anyone who frustrated you or made you uncomfortable, and you may end up cheating yourself out of a quality hire.

HANDLING THE ESPECIALLY QUIET INTERVIEWEE

Some of the same techniques you would use for a nervous interviewee will also work for the shy or quiet candidate. If you find you're getting three-word responses to each question, be specific about what you want the candidate to elaborate on. One technique that can be useful is called **echoing**. If you ask a candidate why he is leaving a current position and he says, "I'm hoping to move my career along and take it to the next level by finding something a little more challenging," you can respond to that by echoing a part of the answer. "So you find your current job unchalleng-ing. Why is that? And what would a more challenging job look like to you?" That invites the candidate to expand on that thought. If getting the person to talk about himself is like pulling teeth throughout the inter-view, you'll have to weigh that factor along with other job criteria.

The overqualified applicant

Be cautious, but don't rule out talent

This candidate looks great on paper, and during the interview she sounds even better. The problem is, the position she's interviewing for could be seen as a step down from the last one she had. Should you be thrilled this person is interested in the job or should you be concerned that she's overqualified?

The fact is, during recessions or tight labor markets, candidates who have been downsized or those who can't afford to be pounding the pavement for more than a few weeks will be eager to get a job they know they can do and earn a steady paycheck. And you certainly don't want to immediately exclude a candidate because he or she has too much talent.

On the other hand, you do want to be cautious; the hire you make today has to last a good long time. Bringing in an outstandingly competent employee won't help you if he leaves for a better position as soon as the economy shows signs of recovery. And, of course, you want someone who will be motivated to contribute on a day-to-day basis and who will feel challenged.

In this scenario, during the interview you'll need to play career counselor and probe into why this person is interested in this position. Be open about your concern. "This job seems to be a step down for you titlewise and salarywise—what's in it for you?" If the candidate acknowledges the issue but says that he would prefer to sacrifice salary and title today for future growth opportunities, then talk about what those might be at your company. Find out more about his long-term career goals and be frank about when you think this person can reasonably expect to be promoted, assuming good performance. You may want to consider expanding the position to include other responsibilities. But never promise anything you can't deliver.

THE UNQUALIFIED
INTERVIEWEE

Occasionally, an underqualified candidate will slip through the résumé screening process; he may have submitted a résumé just vague enough to appear that he had the requisite experience, but on closer inspection doesn't have what it takes. You may realize this in the first few minutes of the interview. So what do you do then? Should you limit the interview to five minutes and then stand up and say, "Thank you for coming by"? Or are you obligated to see it through to the end?

There are a few good reasons to continue. For one thing, you want to cover your bases legally. The moment the candidate walks in, there are a host of physical characteristics you now know about; if the candidate perceives that you've based your decision not to hire him based on anything illegal, this could provide the makings of a case against your company. The complications you could be avoiding are certainly worth a 20- to 30-minute interview with someone you know you won't hire.

For another thing, continuing the interview would be, more or less, the right thing to do, given that you made the appointment and the candidate made the interview a priority.

Finally, you never know where this interview will lead. Some employers, who have explained very professionally and sensitively that they were looking for someone with more or different job experience, have been rewarded with good word-of-mouth public relations or a new customer.

The unemployed candidate

It's not a deal-breaker anymore

Employers used to assume if someone was unemployed, there must be a reason. But times have changed. A stagnant economy can put a lot of talented people on the unemployment line, thanks to layoffs and downsizing. It's also possible that the candidate took a break to start a family or pursue another interest. So be sure to keep an open mind with such candidates, while also being careful to explore all gaps in employment history during the interview.

Your first question should be: "So why did you leave your last job?" If the candidate says he was laid off, along with his or her whole department, ask if you can call the former employer as a reference. If things ended amicably, that shouldn't be a problem. If it is a problem, ask why.

If you get a vague answer to your first question, such as, "Things didn't work out with my last boss," probe until you get to the heart of the matter. If the issue was a personality conflict, it's possible the candidate would make a better fit for you and your company, but you want to know more about what caused the problem.

If the candidate says he left to take some time off and "re-examine things," make sure you get a satisfactory answer about what he came up with. What led him back? What did he learn about himself during that time? Was he otherwise happy at the job he left? If his former employer wanted to rehire him, would he accept? Why or why not? If specific circumstances of his private life caused him to leave his job, find out whether those circumstances have changed.

If the candidate says he left to pursue a freelance or consulting career, focus on what he's been doing since leaving his former employer. Find out why he's decided to go back to the corporate world. If the freelance route wasn't a success, find out why.

ASK THE EXPERTS

If I have two equally qualified candidates, but one is currently employed and the other isn't, should I always choose the former?

Not unless you have other reasons for choosing that person. There are a few strategic advantages to hiring someone who is currently out of work and who may have been jobless for some amount of time. First, they'll be motivated—both to start immediately and to do a great job when they do. Second, you usually won't have the risk of a potential counteroffer that might wreck your deal right at the last stage (though it can happen if the candidate is in demand and is interviewing elsewhere). Third, in general, someone who has been out of work for months will usually demand less salarywise than someone who feels comfortably employed.

EXAMINE THE FREELANCE GIG

It's common to find the title "independent contractor," "freelance consultant," or another variation on the résumé of a candidate who was let go, laid off, or fired. Your job is find out if he really was consulting or contracting, or if that just sounded better than "couch potato." That's relatively easy to do. Someone who has been building his own freelance business will have a list of clients—or at least one or two big ones— whom you can contact for a reference interview. Ask about each job or project the same way you would about any previous job experience. Can the client quantify the candidate's contribution to that company? Are there any finished projects you can look at? Make sure to ask the candidate about his current freelance commitments and how he plans to handle those going forward. You may not mind if he moonlights, but you want to make sure your new hire won't be working for any competitors on the side.

Helpful resources

Tools you can use

BOOKS

How to Read a Person Like a Book
(e-book from Barnes & Noble.com)
by Gerard I. Nierenberg
and Henry H. Calero

The Evaluation Interview
by Richard A. Fear
and Robert J. Chiron

Listening: The Forgotten Skill: A Self-Teaching Guide
by Madelyn Burley-Allen

WEB SITES

"Listening Skills in the Workplace"
www.spring-institute.org/ pdf/ListeningWkplc.pdf
This article from the Spring Institute for International Studies examines the "listening process" and identifies the factors that affect listening. (Requires Adobe Acrobat Reader.)

Setting the Tone
http://www.lrims.com/set_tone. html
Workplace-management consultancy LRI Management Services offers tips to help managers set the tone of the interview "in first 2 minutes."

Vault: EmployerVault
www.vault.com/hubs/302/ hubhome_302.jsp?ch_id=302
This career site for employers offers updated articles, surveys, and plenty of advice for managers. Includes a Q&A with a recruiting expert on "interview manners."

CHAPTER EIGHT

BEYOND THE BASICS

Narrowing it down

Deciding who to bring back for another round

So you've seen your first round of candidates. Good, you're making headway. Hopefully, several good potential new hires have emerged by now.

Now you need to narrow your search to no more than a few front-runners. Depending on your time and how competitive the candidates are, this number might range from two to about five candidates. One way to do this in a methodical fashion is to create a table (see page 133, top box), either by hand or using a software program such as Excel, listing each candidate on the left and key job criteria across the top. For each candidate, put an "x" or checkmark in the box that corresponds with each criterion if they meet it. Even better, rate that candidate on that particular skill on a scale of 1 to 5 or 1 to 10 (see page 133, bottom box), with 5 or 10 being "very qualified." In the sample at bottom, right, for example, based on their higher ratings, you might bring in Sandra, Tom, and Mark for second interviews.

You might also want to create an additional box at the end of each candidate's row. This allows you to jot down your personal observations about character, as well as how well you think he or she would get along with the rest of the team and the company culture.

NO VIABLE CANDIDATES?

If you have no potential hires after the first round of interviewing, you'll need to go back to the pile of résumés that has probably continued to grow in your inbox. A dearth of good prospects early on may indicate a need for reviewing the job posting. You might have to alter the level of experience you want. Instead of asking for five years of experience, for example, you may need to settle for three.

CHECKING IT OFF

Key Criteria	Sandra	Tom	Mark	Lisa	Sue
College degree	X	X		X	
Two yrs + sales experience		X	X		X
Exp in retail sales		X	X		
Knowledge of luxury goods	X		X		
Excellent oral and written communication skills	X	X		X	
Positive, professional attitude	X	X	X	X	X

This simple table gives you an overview of which candidates for a sales position at a luxury retailer possess the greatest number of skills critical to the job.

BASIC RATING OF CANDIDATES

The following candidates have been rated on a scale of 1 to 5 (5=very qualified) to determine how well they fill the job's major requirements.

Key Criteria	Sandra	Tom	Mark	Lisa	Sue
College degree	4	3	0	5	0
Two yrs + sales experience	1	3	4	0	5
Exp in retail sales	0	3	4	0	1
Knowledge of luxury goods	5	2	5	1	1
Excellent oral and written communication skills	5	5	3	5	2
Positive, professional attitude	5	4	5	5	4
TOTAL	20	20	21	16	13

Second interviews

What's left to ask?

Once you've narrowed your pool down to those few candidates you want to bring back for the second interview, call them immediately to let them know they've made the cut and ask them to come in. Again, schedule the interviews close together, within one or two days, if possible; compressing this part of the cycle will help you move toward final selection more quickly and efficiently.

This is often your last meeting with each candidate before selection, so make the most of it and prepare. Prior to meeting with the candidates, review their résumés and your lists of notes on each candidate. Write down any outstanding questions. This is your opportunity to delve more deeply into areas you may have just touched on in the first interview, as well as to fill in missing information.

The second interview would be a good opportunity to discuss skills and aptitude, find out more about any special training he has had or software programs he knows, and whether training would bring him up to speed quickly if he is lacking expertise in some crucial area.

The second interview is also an opportunity to get to know the candidate a little better personally, to get more of a feel for how well this person will fit in with your team, and to gauge how interested he is in the position. If a candidate was overly nervous during the first interview but had the necessary technical skills, now is the time to see if he's over his first-interview jitters. Expect a candidate to have researched the company by the second interview and to have questions for you about the culture and the company's financial stability (see pages 110–111 for how to answer them). Finally, the second interview may include stops at the offices of several other managers from whom you need input (see page 136).

ASK THE EXPERTS

Should I be prepared to make an offer at the end of the second interview?

That depends on how many candidates you are seeing and whether you've already checked references. If you haven't done the latter, you may want to hold off, even if the candidate seems like a perfect fit. If you're concerned about losing that candidate to another bid, be clear about your high level of interest, tell the candidate you'll be deciding very soon, and ask her whether she is considering any other job offers at the moment. That way you let her know an offer is likely, but you give yourself time to confirm everything you've learned about her.

Our timetable doesn't allow for a second interview. Is that a must?

No. But it is something you should know up front, since it will guide your first round of interviews. The second interview tends to be for mid- to high-level positions or for jobs that require a certain level of skills or abilities, which might take more than one meeting to evaluate. If the position you're hiring for is a lower-level job and you feel you were able to confidently narrow your choices in the first round, then skip to reference-checking. But don't hire anyone about whom you have out-standing questions. If time is a factor, then do a follow-up interview by phone.

Meeting other staff

Getting input from potential coworkers, managers, or your boss

In some cases, and particularly for lower-level positions, hiring managers will get carte blanche to hire whomever they deem fit for the job. But in most situations, you'll need to gather some opinions from a higher-level executive, other members of your team, or the candidate's potential coworkers. Certainly, if you own your business, you don't need anyone's permission to make a hire—but you may want to introduce the favorite to those he would be working with to get their input.

There are two great reasons to get feedback from others before extending an offer to a candidate, even if you're not required to do so. First, others on your team may have more of a background in some of the technical skills you're looking for in this candidate, and they may think of important questions to ask that you didn't. Second, getting buy-in from others extends "ownership" of the decision to other people in your group. The greater the number of people who feel they had a role in the new hire, the more the whole team will pull for his success on the job.

That said, you don't want too many colleagues involved in this process, because this can make it hard to reach an agreement. So limit your introductions to those whose sign-on you'll need to make an offer, or to those who will be responsible for training or evaluating the new hire later on. The best time to solicit feedback is after the first or second round of interviewing, when you've had a chance to form an opinion about the candidates and, ideally, to narrow the pool down to one or two top candidates.

You may decide to sit in on the meeting between the colleague and candidate, or you may decide to leave them on their own. Either way, you should sit down with your colleague immediately afterward to go over initial impressions and concerns.

HANDLING A
DIFFERENCE OF OPINION

If you have already decided whom you want to
hire for a position, you are probably considering the
candidate's meeting with your boss to be more a formality than anything
else. But what if you find out your boss really dislikes the candidate you
want to hire, while he loves the candidate you felt only lukewarm about?

Before getting upset, sit down with your boss and find out what kinds
of issues she has with the candidate you selected. She may have found
your candidate's technical knowledge lacking or thinks that the candidate
is missing key experience that you overlooked. This discussion will also
give you a chance to make your case. If the tipping point in your decision
is personality based, for instance, you may want to point out that you will
be working with this person on a daily basis, whereas your boss will see
that person only monthly. If you feel your favored candidate would fit in
with the culture of your team, that is something your boss should value.

At the same time, be careful not to push too hard for a candidate your
boss isn't crazy about, since that may cause her to watch the new hire
closely, and the employee's performance will reflect squarely on you. Your
goal is to sell your manager on your selection, but if that can't be done
comfortably, you might want to consider moving on to another candidate.

Requiring a presentation

If public speaking and making presentations are job requirements, it might make sense to have your top candidates give a presentation as part of the second interview. Typically, you would give the candidate a topic to present and a few days to prepare it. This is a good hands-on way of testing the applicant's skills and knowledge, specifically:

Public speaking skills
Many jobs involve making presentations, whether internally to other departments or externally to vendors, clients, investors, or the public.

The image that the applicant portrays
That image will be linked to the organization whenever and wherever he is present.

The candidate's thinking and writing abilities
Good presentations follow a logical order of thought, so pay attention to how well the applicant structures the presentation.

Some hiring managers do not give candidates advance notice about making a presentation, and give that person only 15 to 30 minutes to prepare at the second-round interview. They may do this to see how well the applicants perform under pressure and how well they speak extemporaneously. Use this tactic, however, only if the position requires these kinds of high-pressure speaking skills; otherwise, you're liable to upset the candidate and give her a negative impression of you and your company. It is almost always best to give the candidates some preparation time rather than springing this kind of thing on them.

Note that for other kinds of positions, particularly creative ones, different kinds of short tasks may be appropriate, such as having a programmer write a short section of code or having a graphic design applicant come up with a sample ad.

PRESENTATION GUIDELINES

If you decide to have the top candidates give presentations, be sure to provide them with all the details they need to do a good job. These include:

Time

Usually 5 to 15 minutes should suffice. If you want to include a Q&A period, decide upon a length of time to allot for it, and make sure the candidate knows about it.

Topic

Be clear about whether you are going to provide a specific topic, or if you are going to leave the topic up to the candidate.

Context

Some hiring managers like to provide an imaginary context for a presentation—for example, a speech aimed at a major client or new employees.

Visual aids

Make sure the candidate knows what is expected and what technology and equipment is available, such as PowerPoint or a flip chart.

Hard copies

Be clear about whether you want the candidate to provide printouts of the visuals and/or script, and let him know how many copies to make.

Facilities

Choose an appropriate space for the presentation, either the spot where actual presentations take place or one that is similar. Take some care in setting up the room to mimic a real presentation, and to provide any necessary equipment, such as a laptop computer or microphone.

Offsite meetings

When an outing can help

Interviews at corporate headquarters or at the location for which you're hiring are certainly standard—at least for the first interview. But offsite lunch meetings have grown significantly in popularity. They boomed in the mid '90s as entrepreneurs wooed young hot-shot techies via expensive lunches and dinners.

Meeting a candidate at a local restaurant gives you a chance to see him in a more relaxed, casual setting. Someone who may be nervous or awkward sitting across a desk might warm up a bit over a plate of pasta or over coffee and pastries at a local café. You'll likely learn more about him personally through a casual conversation than you would in the formal structure of an office interview.

If you are interviewing for a sales position or any other position that will involve lunch meetings, the offsite meal is almost a must. You wouldn't want to hire someone and have your clients or customers see a side of your employee that you hadn't already previewed. That isn't to say you should be fixing an eagle gaze on which fork she uses for the salad, but, at the same time, you want to get a sense of the person's people skills, how comfortable she feels when not behind a desk, whether she has good basic etiquette—that sort of thing. It's a good idea to stay away from alcohol; you want to have your wits about you when evaluating the candidate.

On the downside, taking notes during a lunch meeting can be awkward, which means you'll have to take good mental notes on the information you get. If it seems unlikely you'll retain much, keep a small notepad on your lap or near your plate so you can jot things down quickly.

ASK THE EXPERTS

I'm bringing five people back for a second interview. Do I have to take every one to lunch individually?

That will depend on how interested you are in each of them—and what the limit is on your expense account. Make sure you know up front how much you can spend on this stage of the recruiting process, and stay within budget. If time and expense are not factors, and you are equally impressed with each of the five, feel free to break bread with all of them. Otherwise, limit lunches to the two or three favorites in the group.

At a lunch interview, I found my favorite candidate for a sales position to be a bit unpolished. Is that enough to disqualify him?

That depends on the position and how heavily you weigh etiquette. It's a subjective thing, and you have to imagine what your clients would think. But if you really like the candidate, and the breaches are minimal, there are ways to deal with it that don't require rejecting the candidate. There are seminars, for example, that offer basic etiquette training for executives.

Long-distance interviews

When the candidate comes to you

During second-round interviews, you may want to bring a long-distance candidate, whom you've probably interviewed only over the phone, to company headquarters. If you plan to do so, make sure to work out all of the details concerning cost, transportation, and lodging ahead of time.

Most employers do not expect candidates to pay for out-of-town travel expenses such as airfare and hotels. However, if travel is fairly local (within an hour's drive), it's not uncommon to require candidates to pay their own taxi, bus, or gas expenses. But make sure you discuss this in advance with the candidate.

Some other things to be aware of when requiring candidates to travel to you for an interview:

Agree on expenses up front

It is important to agree who will pay for what before the candidate travels. What companies pay for varies widely; for example, some organizations include a per diem allowance, while others don't. It also depends on how badly you want to recruit the candidate. If the person is your ideal pick, then don't be afraid to pull out all the stops, if you can afford it, to make the candidate's trip comfortable and pleasant.

Clarify the process

Many organizations ask candidates to work through a travel agency it uses or through an internal travel department. In either case, airfare, car service, and hotels are often arranged and paid for directly by the company hosting the candidate. However, it's common to ask the candidate to put hotel fees on his credit card and to reimburse him later. Food, aside from interview meals, is not usually covered by the host.

Ask the candidate to save receipts

These are necessary for reimbursement purposes and to prepare an expense summary after the trip.

Pricey surprise

"Last year I had to hire an account manager for our national advertising agency. This was the first time I had hired anyone, and I guess I didn't get all the information I needed up front about what our company pays for if we bring in candidates from other cities. I thought I had settled all the details with a candidate we flew in from Illinois, but boy was I wrong. She evidently assumed that we would pay for personal phone calls from her hotel room, as well as for minibar snacks and alcohol. You can imagine how surprised I was when I received the receipt for her stay—and saw that she had racked up $75 in calls to her boyfriend! Not only that, but her minibar bill alone was almost $50. My boss certainly wasn't pleased that I had not worked these details out with her beforehand. Next time, I will definitely make sure each candidate has a list of what our company can and cannot reimburse for before I fly anyone out and put them up in a hotel."

David B., Phoenix, AZ

Videoconferencing

Companies are increasingly turning to **videoconferencing** to screen candidates. This sophisticated technology allows companies to avoid travel costs by connecting you and the interviewee via a monitor, microphone, and video cable.

This is great if you wouldn't otherwise be able to meet a potential candidate, but videoconferencing can be a little tricky. There's often a transmission delay and an echo that make conversation awkward. Voices may overlap. You can't move around or you'll find yourself out of the camera's range. But don't let this worry you. There are some tried-and-true ways to make your end of the video interview run smoothly:

Prepare ahead of time

In addition to the general preparation you need to do before holding an interview, you have to consider how the presence of a camera is going to affect things. Set the agenda ahead of time and make sure the candidate knows what to expect, then get used to the process by practicing some of your questions in front of a mirror or home video camera.

Keep it brief

A videoconference interview is not always as flexible as a face-to-face interview. Because of the slight time delay, it often does not have the easy give-and-take of an in-person dialogue. Keep your questions and comments short. At the same time, don't hesitate to prompt for information if the answer to your question is not detailed enough.

LIGHTS, CAMERA, ACTION!

If you've ever been on TV you're a step ahead of others when it comes to videoconferencing. If this is your first time doing an interview by video, don't let the presence of a camera distract you. Try to concentrate not on the fact that you are being viewed on a screen by the interviewee, but on the content of the interview itself. Here are some other ways to come across effectively on-screen:

Dress simply

Solid primary colors work best. Don't wear blue or white: Both can disappear on-screen and leave you looking like a disembodied head. Avoid patterned clothing because it can "zigzag" on camera.

Do not wear jewelry that glitters or makes noise

If you normally wear eyeglasses, try to do the interview without them, or wear contact lenses. The lenses in eyeglasses can reflect light and make it hard for a candidate to see your eyes.

Wear makeup

Even if you don't normally wear makeup, do try to wear a bit because a camera washes out facial features.

Become familiar with the equipment

Before you begin, test the microphone. Make sure the lights are as bright as possible so that the image will be clear. Ask to be shot from the waist up so that the viewer gets a good view of your face.

Speak directly to the camera

Avoid looking up, down, or to the side; it distracts the viewer.

Remain still. Sit with both feet on the floor and hands resting on a table so that you are well grounded. Try not to use too many hand gestures, to tap your feet impatiently, etc.

Speak slowly and clearly.

Wait until a question is answered completely before starting the next one, because the time delay can throw things off.

Helpful resources

Tools you can use

BOOKS

Everything Job Interview Book
by Bob Adams

*Essential Managers:
Interviewing Skills*
by Tim Hindle

*Recruiting, Interviewing, Selecting
and Orienting New Employees*
by Diane Arthur

WEB SITES

HR Press
**www.hrpress-software.com/
smarthire.html**
This site offers a number of HR software
packages, including SmartHire, a
Windows-based system to manage the
interview, evaluation, and selection
process for new hires.

About.com's Career Center
**http://jobsearch.about.com/
library/weekly/aa110401a.htm**
This article examines the dos and don'ts of
dining etiquette while on an interview.
Good for interviewers as well as
interviewees.

*CheckStart Candidate Comparison
Worksheet*
**www.checkstart.com/about/
cand_comparison_wksht.html**
Features a sample of a candidate rating
sheet for managers from Psichometrics,
LLC, a firm specializing in behavioral and
cognitive interviewing.

CHAPTER NINE

CHECKING REFERENCES

The checking process

By now you've likely narrowed down the candidate pool to just a few front-runners, which brings you to perhaps the most important stage of the hiring process: checking references.

It also happens to be the step most often overlooked. Too many managers (and prospective employees, for that matter) have come to think of reference-checking as a formality, something you're required to check off the list, but not anything you expect to really influence or interfere with the decision you make. In fact, many managers will make an informal offer to a candidate before checking references—"Assuming your references check out, we're ready to make you an offer"—which invariably puts them in an awkward spot should they discover anything that would sour them on the new hire. And because they feel as though it's a done deal, they treat their reference interviews as afterthoughts and miss asking the probing questions that would help them learn more about the person they may decide to bring aboard.

Of course, it's easy to want to trust a candidate you've come to like; psychologically speaking, checking references can feel like you're checking up on the person because you think he's lying to you. While most candidates don't lie, a few do embellish the facts on their résumés and in interviews. Instead of trying to suss out any exaggerators, put your mind to rest and check into previous job experience by asking a third party who should have knowledge of it.

Consider it a service to the candidate as well. Many people have trouble speaking highly about themselves in interviews, but a former employer who enjoyed working with that person will be happy to list the many ways she contributed to the organization's success. You may learn things you didn't know before that make the candidate even better for the job, giving you greater confidence in your decision.

ASK THE EXPERTS

The position I'm hiring for is a fairly low-level one. Do I still need to check references?

Absolutely. Every employee is in a position to contribute to—or detract from—your company's productivity. And every one of them has some sort of professional track record. If you're hiring a cashier, for example, you need to know if this person is trustworthy and friendly and has the right attitude for greeting customers. The best person to ask is a former employer.

How recent should the reference be?

Generally speaking, references should be able to comment on the candidate's job performance sometime over the past seven years. Beyond that, there isn't that much value. A person can gain quite a bit of experience in that amount of time, and chances are the candidate was not sufficiently experienced 10 years ago for the job you're interviewing for now.

DO YOUR PREP WORK BEFOREHAND

Like candidate interviews, reference interviews are most effective when you have adequately prepared and allotted the time for them. Unprepared, you are more apt to ask references canned, generic questions that yield equally generic responses. Avoid leading questions; for example, "So Sally was very helpful with customers then?" That's not as likely to give you as useful an answer as: "How would you grade Sally's ability to handle queries from dissatisfied customers?"

Before calling any references, sit down with the candidate's résumé and interview notes and consider carefully what you really want to check. Prepare a list of questions. Allow adequate time with each reference. Somewhere between 10 and 30 minutes is probably the most you'll get, but make sure you've blocked out between 30 and 60 minutes in case a reference feels particularly talkative.

Whom to contact

Don't wait until you've made the job offer

If you did pre-interview reference checking (see page 82), you already have some basic information about education level, degrees earned, and job titles. If not, now is the time to contact universities and previous employers' HR departments to confirm periods of employment. Don't contact any current employers unless you have permission from the candidate. (You can, however, confirm that he works at a current job without rousing suspicion by simply calling the company and asking the receptionist for a telephone number or mailing address for the candidate without giving away who you are.)

The candidate should provide you with a list of at least three references—the more the better, since some may be unavailable when you call. The list should include names, companies, titles, mailing addresses, telephone numbers, and e-mail addresses. They should be primarily professional references, unless you specifically feel you might gain from speaking with personal references, such as a former professor or a supervisor at a volunteer organization. Steer clear of friends and family. Of course, if the candidate comes to you from another department or regional division within your company, you should start by contacting the supervisor there.

Other potential references will depend on the position for which you're hiring. If it involves working very interactively on a team, it would be useful to speak with peers or colleagues who have worked with the candidate in the past five years, though not in a supervisory role. They would be in the best position to comment on the candidate's cooperation skills and spirit of collegiality.

ASK THE EXPERTS

Are there any situations in which a candidate would want me to contact their current employer?

Yes, there are cases in which an employee will talk to a supervisor about wanting to make a change or move in another direction and the supervisor will understand and try to help. There are other cases, however, where the employee isn't working out and the employer is helping the person as an alternative to firing him. Be aware of that possibility and when you talk to the employer, try to assess the situation tactfully.

USE YOUR INGENUITY TO CHECK IN OTHER WAYS

The references provided by the candidate are a good start, but don't feel limited to them. After all, they may be useful in your assessment, but the candidate may have coached them to provide glowing recommendations. Do your own research to find objective sources, and include anyone to whom your candidate reported in the past (except for his current employer). Focus specifically on immediate supervisors, since they will be the best sources for reliable information. If the candidate lists any industry associations on his résumé or mentions any informal industry networks he belongs to, ask around at these organizations too. Ask the references with whom you speak for the names of any others whom the candidate has worked with.

Remember: Before speaking to anyone who is not on the list of references provided by the candidate, inform the applicant of your intentions to contact those people, so you avoid any legal issues later on. Ideally, you should have the candidate sign a waiver or disclosure-authorization form acknowledging that you'll be talking to industry colleagues and giving you permission to talk to anyone who could shed light on past professional behavior. And realize that some you contact may not want to say anything because of fear of legal reprisal (see page 160).

Get the conversation started

So you're ready to do a reference check. How do you go about it? First, plan to contact the reference by telephone, rather than seeking a response via mail or e-mail. Written recommendations will tell you only what the reference wants to share, rather than what you specifically need to know.

When you reach the reference source on the phone, introduce yourself, offering your name, title, and company. Explain that you are considering the candidate for a position with your company. If you're calling a reference that was provided by the candidate, make sure to say explicitly that the candidate led you to him. That can often put a jittery source at ease. If the source wasn't on the candidate's list, explain how you wound up calling her and why you think her input would be valuable.

Before asking any questions, give the reference some context for her answers by providing an overview of your company's culture—whether it's a less structured start-up-company that doesn't do a lot of handholding or a large corporation that needs employees who can follow rules and procedures. If you're concerned that too much information will bias the answers—particularly in a case where the source is a big fan of the candidate—keep the background more general and offer only a broad description of the position you're filling.

Be sure to keep a friendly, collegial tone. If you sound formal and anxious, the person on the other end will feel that way too, but if you sound relaxed and comfortable, chances are you will put her at ease. And the more relaxed the person is, the better her information will be.

REFERENCE CHECKING TIPS

- Prepare a list of questions ahead of time.

- Leave yourself plenty of time for the phone call and make sure you won't be disturbed.

- If you delegate any reference calls, make sure it's to a trained reference checker, and interview at least one source yourself.

- Assure the reference that anything he says about the candidate will be kept in strictest confidence.

- Check all dates and times during which the candidate claims to have worked with the reference.

- Keep the questions strictly job related, and pose the same or similar questions to each reference.

- If the reference wants to keep talking, let him do so and try to "listen between the lines." If you hear something vaguely negative—or a backward compliment—probe for more.

- Take copious notes during each reference interview.

- Do your best *not* to form quick opinions based on the first reference.

Asking tough questions

Getting the most out of your reference check

After getting the easy questions out of the way—dates of employment, titles, basic job responsibilities—you'll move on to the evaluation phase of the interview. Here you have a few options. If the reference is particularly talkative, relaxed, and forthcoming, you might ask him to rate the candidate's skills, performance, work ethic, enthusiasm, etc., on a scale of 1 to 10. The advantage of a rating system is that by asking each reference the same questions, you wind up with hard numbers you can add up to get a final rating and a general picture of how well the candidate would perform in your environment. The downside of a rating system is that it's subjective, and if you rely on the numbers alone, you might not get an accurate picture. Make sure to ask the reference to give each rating a detailed explanation, and to provide examples.

Another option is to develop questions that offer a choice of two answers. For example: "Some employees are always eager to take on more job responsibility and do so without being asked, while others choose to stick to the tasks they are assigned. Which style would you say best describes Sally?" This can be a big help to those who seem uncomfortable talking or who don't know quite what you're looking for; this way they can tell you a lot in very few words.

If the reference is particularly quiet or seems not to want to elaborate, ask him to at least confirm statements you have about the candidate. For example, "Joe says he was directly responsible for order fulfillment in your division. Is that true?"

Remember: Don't shy away from the tough questions, particularly when talking to references who were not on the candidate's list. The most informative answers are usually in response to the questions you least want to ask, such as how well the candidate handles authority, or how much work time the candidate spends on personal matters.

SAMPLE QUESTIONS FOR REFERENCE

- When did the candidate start/stop working for you?

- What was his or her title?

- What were his or her responsibilities and duties?

- What were the candidate's areas of strength?

- In what areas did he or she need improvement?

- How does the candidate respond to last-minute changes in schedule or unexpected crises?

- How well does the candidate "put out fires" at work?

- What kinds of people would you say the candidate had the most trouble interacting with?

- How early/late did the candidate arrive/leave work?

- How many hours a week did it take the candidate to do his or her job?

- How does the candidate compare to the employee currently doing his or her job?

- How would you rate the candidate's ability to accept constructive criticism?

- How would you describe his or her ability to incorporate that criticism going forward?

- How well developed are the candidate's time-management skills? Listening skills?

- How would you describe your management style and how did the candidate mesh with that?

- Why did the candidate leave the company? (If it was the result of a layoff, how many other people were laid off at that time?)

- Would you rehire the candidate? If not, why not?

Evaluating the information

Create a level playing field by asking everyone the same questions

Asking each reference the same questions about a former employee's performance makes it easy to cross-check information. If you get wildly different responses from two former supervisors, for example, that's a red flag—particularly if the positive reference you got came from someone the candidate suggested, while the negative review came from a source you uncovered yourself.

Keep in mind, however, that references can have axes to grind as well. Although, for example, a candidate might have left a former employer because work conditions were intolerable or because the boss took advantage by making him work weekends without compensation, that employer may not view things that way, and so may not be the most reliable source.

Since you promised confidentiality to your sources, you can't then go back to the candidate and share the source of a negative review with him to get his side of things. What you can do is use your judgment after tallying the responses. If you got one negative review out of four interviews with previous supervisors, you have to decide how much weight to give that one opinion. While interviewing, be sure to probe a negative comment and ask for concrete examples of the bad behavior or poor attitude. Find out if the candidate was warned or disciplined while working there. Listen for hesitations on the other end of the line or for overly terse responses; in other words, be attuned not only to what the reference says, but to what she does not say.

ASK THE EXPERTS

What if the reference wants to communicate via e-mail?

E-mail, while a great corporate communication tool, isn't ideal for reference-checking. While it can be somewhat interactive, you can miss out on some key features—such as tone of voice or hesitation before answering. If time is an issue for the source, ask the reference to spare just 10 minutes on the phone, and then use your time wisely.

What kind of information am I not allowed to check into?

According to the law you cannot access school records, medical files, or psychiatric files without explicit written permission from the candidate. You can verify degrees without consent, however, and that's really all you need.

FIRST PERSON INSIGHTS
Trusting your instincts

"I called a former employer who was not on the list of references the candidate gave me. The candidate had been very open with me about the situation in our interview and why things had ended unpleasantly; instinctively, I believed her, but I wanted to get the employer's side to be sure. What I got was an earful of negative comments. I wasn't sure whom to believe, but instinctively I decided to check up on the reference via some industry connections—and found out that this particular manager had a reputation for working his people to the bone, and that his department had a high rate of turnover. Finding out that the reference was probably one-sided gave me that extra measure of confidence to hire the candidate."

Rakim B., Louisville, KY

Credit checks

These days it's becoming more and more common for employers to do **credit checks** on prospective employees, particularly on those who will be handling money or will have access to small valuable items, like jewelry or electronics. Employers also sometimes do credit checks on employees who will be entering homes to provide a service, such as shampooing rugs or caring for the elderly.

These employers feel that a credit report showing irresponsible money management or large debt should be a warning sign. If a candidate can't manage his own money, how well can you expect him to handle yours? Other employers worry that a candidate with a lot of debt may have more incentive to steal.

If any of these concerns have crossed your mind, and you run a business in which an employee's financial situation might affect job performance, make sure to cross all your legal t's before you decide to run a report.

Employers are only allowed to do credit reports and use them to make hiring decisions if there is a very good reason why this information is necessary for the job. Additionally, a potential employee must agree in writing beforehand if you want to run a credit check.

If you do allow a credit report to influence your hiring decision, have good reasons ready to back up your decision in case the candidate wants to know what the problem was.

ASK THE EXPERTS

I did a credit check on our top candidate for an accounting position and was alarmed to see a history of late and skipped credit-card payments. Should I discuss this with him up front?

Yes. If there's any reason why his credit report makes you hesitate to hire him, do discuss this with him. He may have a good explanation for what is on the report. An ex-spouse may have run up their joint credit cards. He may have had a serious illness and insufficient insurance to cover his bills. Any number of things could have happened. But it may also be that he has a hard time managing his money. Whatever the case may be, give him a chance to explain. You might say: "I see from your credit report that there have been some issues with payments in the past. Do you feel comfortable explaining to me what this is about?"

Troubleshooting

Coping with reluctant sources

Usually managers will have no problem getting references—at least those on a candidate's list—to talk to them. However, some may be reluctant to talk, especially references who were not on that list.

The reason behind this? Fear of legal reprisal, which has become more widespread at some companies in recent years. Former employers may not want to say anything negative or positive, but particularly negative, about a former employee for fear of being sued for **character defamation**. And some companies have even instituted policies allowing you to verify only the most basic information, such as name, dates of employment, and positions held.

That can put you in a bit of a pickle, since you should always do a thorough reference check before hiring anyone. In response to this problem, many states have passed laws in recent years making it easier for former employers to talk openly with a candidate's prospective employer. Generally, this legislation says that companies providing reference information in "good faith" are protected from defamation suits. This right to pass on information is also known as "qualified privilege."

But the changes to many states' laws haven't eliminated all the fear associated with references, so you may find some sources turning down your request. Make it a point to let them know about the law if it applies to your state; don't assume that all the references you are contacting know about your state's relaxed laws on qualified privilege. If you don't know what your state's laws are concerning this, ask your HR or legal department or call your state's Department of Labor.

BACKGROUND CHECKS:
GETTING IT IN WRITING

To supplement the reference information you get, you may need or want to hire a company to do a background check. Basic checks can run you anywhere from $25 to $150 per search, and will include a rundown on criminal history, a motor vehicle report, and verification of Social Security information. You can add on components such as verification of employment history, education, and military history. Before beginning any such investigation, you must first have the candidate sign an **Employment Inquiry Release form**. There are longer forms for comprehensive checks, which you can obtain from your HR department.

Here is a sample of a short form:

This document authorizes Widgets, Inc., to make investigative background inquiries in connection with my possible employment with Widgets, Inc. I understand that these background inquiries will include, but will not be limited to, consumer, criminal, driving, and other reports, and will include information regarding my character, work habits, performance, and experience, including reasons for termination of past employment. I understand, further, that Widgets may be requesting information from various federal, state, and other agencies that maintain records concerning my past activities relating to my driving, credit, criminal, and other experiences, as well as claims involving me in the files of insurance companies.

In compliance with the Fair Credit Reporting Act, I am entitled to be informed if an offer of employment is withheld due to information obtained during any of the above inquiries and, upon my request, Widgets will provide a copy of the report along with the FTC notice "A Summary of Your Rights Under the Fair Credit Reporting Act."

I authorize, without reservation, any part or agency contacted by this employer to furnish the above-mentioned information.

Candidate's Name _____

Address _____

Social Security Number _____

Driver's License Number _____

Candidate's Signature _____

Helpful resources

Tools you can use

BOOKS

The Complete Reference Checking Handbook: The Proven (and Legal) Way to Prevent Hiring Mistakes
by Edward C. Andler and Dara Herbst

Reference Checking for Everyone: How to Find Out Everything You Need to Know about Anyone
by Paul Barada

Legal, Effective References: How to Give and Get Them
by Wendy Bliss

Hiring Smart: How to Conduct Background Checks
by Philip D. Dickinson

WEB SITES

Alliant Diagnostics
www.alliantdiagnostics.com
This firm, based in Boca Raton, Florida, offers extensive background-investigation and employment-verification services.

Employment Screening Services
www.esrcheck.com/ESR Publications/Reference_ Checking.htm
A primer on reference-checking from Employment Screening Resources, which also offers screening for employers.

Workforce Management
www.workforce.com/ section/06/feature/23/51/30/ index.html
A guide to successful reference-checking, from *Workforce Management* magazine online.

CHAPTER TEN

MAKING THE HIRE

A close race

Lucky you—your candidate search has yield two exceptional prospects. Your only problem is that you can't decide between them! Now what? Before deciding it with a coin toss, ask yourself a few questions to try and narrow it down:

Which one seemed the better fit for your company culture?
While technical skills and experience go the furthest in job success, the next most important criterion is the candidate's ability to flourish in your organization's environment.

Which one would benefit most from your management style?
This one requires you to get inside the candidates' heads for a moment and, judging from their interview responses and personalities, determine which one would respond most positively to your management style. If your tendency is to be somewhat abrupt or overly assertive and one of the candidates seems to be sensitive and reserved while the other appears to have a thicker skin, the former might not perform to his greatest potential under your management, and you wouldn't be doing him a service by hiring him.

Which one did you like the best?
You'll probably be working closely with this person. Assuming the candidates have equal aptitude, choose the person with whom you feel you will be most comfortable.

Having two worthy candidates is a great position to be in. Just be careful not to be so indecisive that you delay the decision-making process—you don't want your candidates to make the choice for you.

WHEN IN DOUBT, WRITE IT DOWN

Trying to decide between two equally qualified candidates can be intimidating. Sometimes the best way to sort it out is to get it down on paper. First, consult the skill table you made during the interview stage, or if you didn't make it then, now is the perfect time (see page 133). Which candidate had the highest score? The highest weighted score? Take another look at how you weighted the criteria. Would you make any changes? If you did, would it affect either of the candidate's scores, putting one in front of the other? If you wind up with equal scores after a second look (and you may want to do this even if you don't), try the old-fashioned "pros and cons" list. This will give you a chance to list things you liked and didn't like about the candidates that wouldn't end up on a list of criteria but that are nevertheless important to you.

FIRST PERSON INSIGHTS
Enthusiasm wins the day

"A few years back, I had to decide between two equally qualified candidates for the position of public relations assistant. On paper, it was almost impossible to distinguish between them, and their interviews were both impressive. I decided to have another brief chat with each of the candidates, and this time I noticed that one of them was highly enthusiastic about the prospect of joining our firm, while from the other, I got the impression that it wasn't his dream job. In the end, I realized the openly eager candidate would be the better choice for us. Because she was excited and felt this would be a great opportunity for her, I figured she was more likely to be happy and productive on the job, and less likely to be looking for other opportunities. And I was right. That employee flourished in our environment and is now assistant manager of our firm."

Ellen K., Billings, MT

Counteroffers

It's a scenario feared by hiring managers everywhere: You finally make that tough decision and select one of the candidates for employment. You make an offer; the candidate accepts, and you relax in the knowledge that in a few weeks you'll have a new pair of hands on deck.

But the next day the employee calls back to tell you that when she gave notice, her boss made her a **counteroffer** of a promotion, a raise, and a bonus to keep her. How could she possibly pass that up, especially when it's what she really wanted all along? You've effectively secured a promotion and a raise for your candidate at her current company—and you have lost your top candidate!

Sound scary? Relax. You can do a lot to avoid this predicament. The key is to anticipate it early. Ask the candidate during the interview what it would take for her to be happy at her current place of employment. If she cites factors other than salary, such as added benefits, career advancement, a change of industry, she will likely be less interested in a counteroffer.

In your offer meeting, discuss the scenario openly. Ask the candidate if she expects a counteroffer when she resigns and what she would say to it. If she says she has never considered that possibility, you may have reason to be worried. You can rest easier if, instead, you hear this: "I've considered that and thought about my response. At this point, I have too many concerns about my future at my current company and my ability to progress there. I don't feel it's the best environment for me, so even if they were to offer me what you're offering, I would decline."

Candidates seldom know exactly how they will feel in response to a strong counteroffer until it happens. But the more you know up front, the better prepared you'll be.

BIDDING WARS

Say a candidate does get a counteroffer and asks if you're willing to up the ante a little. Should you do it? The first question, of course, is, can you afford to? Assuming you calculated the budget for the position and offered the top amount, then obviously that's all you can afford to pay. If you have a range, however, and you offered the lower end of it, it's possible you could afford to offer a little more, as long as the number is still in your range. But that said, you don't really want to get involved in a bidding war. After all, if you thought the candidate was worth a certain amount, you would have offered it when you made the offer. And you don't want to make it sound like you were holding out because you thought he couldn't do any better.

If you do decide to match in some way, tell the candidate you need a day to consider it. Then come back and reiterate some of the other key benefits you offer the candidate that he isn't getting at the current employer, and say what you are willing to do—perhaps a sign-on bonus or extra vacation time. If that doesn't do it, you may have to move on to the next candidate.

TOP SIGNS A CANDIDATE IS VULNERABLE TO A COUNTEROFFER

1. He's motivated primarily by money. He may say he's looking for greater responsibility or a "change," but in fact he wants higher numbers on his paycheck. You can't blame him, but be prepared to lose him to an aggressive counteroffer.

2. He's accepted a counteroffer in the past. (You learned this when he was explaining why he stayed in the job so long.) If so, he's more likely to repeat the move than those who have turned one down.

3. It's his first major career move. Candidates who haven't made a real jump yet are more susceptible to the security of a counteroffer. They might rather stay with a known employer than risk a new one.

Negotiating pay

The art of the deal

Negotiating pay can be a tricky part of the hiring process—both for hiring managers and for candidates. Given that emotions and expectations can run high, you want to keep as much drama out of the process as possible so you can bring the new hire in for a soft landing.

The best way to prepare for negotiations is to do a little background research ahead of time:

Know the previous salary or range the candidate is anticipating

One way to handle this is to put the range or the salary cap out there in the job advertisement; that way candidates know through the entire process what they can expect when it comes time for the offer. Another way is to insist on salary history in the cover letter submitted with the résumé. This can be tricky because the candidate may include his or her current salary without giving expectations. In any case, salary expectations should be covered early on in the process, during the telephone screening or initial interview.

Understand your company's policies regarding internal equity

You may have some leeway on salary, but your company may have a policy that no new employee can make X percent more than others currently employed who have the same title or job responsibilities. In this case, giving the new guy too much of a bump could create friction.

Be open and honest

Rather than simply saying, "Anne, we're prepared to offer you a salary of $55,000," give a greater context: "Anne, we've looked at our budget for the position as well as the salaries of other employees at the same level. We've also considered your job experience and skills, and we've determined that $55,000 is a fair offer." In that one statement, you've communicated respect and have shown the candidate that you haven't just arbitrarily assigned a figure.

HANDLING THE CANDIDATE
WHO WANTED MORE

For a manager eager to get a new employee on
the payroll, it can be disappointing if a candidate is
less than thrilled with the offer. The first thing to
remember: Don't get emotional. The candidate's reaction isn't personal.
He's simply trying to secure a fair wage. Keep your cool and try to find out
what the candidate was expecting. If, for example, you gave the position a
general range of anywhere from $40,000 to $50,000—or the candidate
gave that as the range he was looking for—and then you offered $42,000,
the candidate may feel let down. He wasn't privy to the confluence of factors impacting your decision, and he may feel you're just trying to get
away with offering the least you can.

Assuming that's not what you were doing, tell the candidate you understand that he might have been expecting the high end of the range and
then explain what went into the decision—budget, level of experience,
internal equity, etc. If you are flexible on salary, ask the candidate what
he's looking for and then take a day or two to think about it and to speak
with any managers who need to weigh in. The trouble with increasing
salary is that it begs the question: If you had more money for the position
and you value this candidate, why didn't you offer it to begin with?
Another option is to say that you're willing to negotiate some of the other
pieces of the compensation pie (see page 36).

Negotiating perks

Generally, candidates care most about high wages. But the **compensation package** isn't all about salary, and employers do themselves a disservice to focus on that alone. Particularly when you know you can't offer a high salary, be prepared to discuss other benefits to sweeten the deal. Certain offerings, like child care options or a subsidized health club membership, can genuinely enhance a candidate's quality of life, and for some this will be as attractive as a salary hike. And then there are the perks, which you can maneuver to your advantage when a salary raise isn't an option (see page 36). The following is a short list.

Title You may not think much of titles—and they may not even mean that much at your company—but your new hire might thrill to a loftier title, figuring it as a way to be better positioned for future career growth. If you can do it without ruffling any feathers internally, consider it a point of negotiation.

Vacation time If a starting employee is entitled only to one week's vacation, and it will take him or her a full year to earn another, offering an additional week up front is a real draw. Note: Company vacation policy shouldn't be broken lightly, since it may not stay under wraps and could cause resentment among the ranks. Make sure the headaches that may result are worth using this as a bargaining chip.

Relocation costs Large companies tend to have set policies about relocation costs, but if you're a smaller organization or you can afford to be flexible on that point, you can effectively increase a relocating employee's first-year salary by paying for moving expenses.

Telecommuting options Not all jobs are set up for **telecommuting**, but many are—and more than some managers think. If transportation cost is an issue for the candidate, you can boost her weekly take-home by allowing one or two days of telecommuting once she demonstrates her reliability and independence.

LONG- AND SHORT-TERM INCENTIVES

If your new candidate is more impressed with dollars and cents than titles and comp time, you may have a few other options open to you (as long as it will not create any tension with existing employees). These include:

A signing bonus

These up-front incentives have been particularly popular in times of labor shortage, but there's no law on when you can offer them. Just make sure you add a contingency clause in writing; for example, the employee gets $5,000 up front, but must stay with the company for at least one year.

Performance bonus

You can guarantee the new hire a **performance bonus** of at least X percent, and possibly more, depending on how he performs, at the end of one year. Remember to document any performance achievements that make the person eligible for a bonus so there are no conflicts later on.

A performance review held earlier than is typical

Suppose you can't afford to increase salary right now, but you could six months from now, assuming the employee merits a raise. The employee knows that instead of having to wait a year to be reviewed, she will have the opportunity for advancement in half that time.

Stock options

These heavily used inducements of the dot-com era are still valuable, even if the stock market isn't what it was. Employees tend to work harder and feel a greater sense of involvement in the company when they own a piece of its future. They also tend to stick around longer because their options can only be exercised after a certain number of years with the company. Most public company stock–option plans have some flexibility regarding the number of options that can be offered to new employees. Check with HR and find out how you can use it to make your new hire happier.

Employment contracts

Making it legal

In cases where the employee is particularly valuable to the organization or in a high-level position—where losing that person will mean a significant loss to the company—you may want her to commit, on paper, to staying for a definite period of time. You never can tell when the next talent war will heat up and you don't want to lose your most valuable employees to a high-bidding competitor out to raid your ranks. An **employment contract** guarantees the minimum duration of the job. It also can address a number of other issues you may want clarified in writing, such as:

The employee's responsibilities Having performance standards and expectations for the job, as well as grounds for termination, spelled out in a contract is like having insurance for the future. If expectations aren't being met, it will be that much easier to let that person go.

Noncompete limitations You can protect the company's intellectual property by including a statement specifying the company's ownership of material or products created by the employee for the company. Some companies have a separate form for this (see page 176). Ask your HR department or an HR lawyer for details.

Agreed-upon bonuses and other future incentives You can specify these in the employment contract to eliminate confusion later.

On the downside, having a contract that specifies duration of the job locks you in as well. If the contract says, for example, that the employee will be with you for three years and you decide after six months that he or she is not working out or if circumstances at the company change, you're essentially stuck. You'll have to renegotiate the contract, and the employee will have the upper hand. Before creating this or any legally binding document, consult a corporate attorney or outside legal counsel to find the best course of action.

WHAT GOES IN AN EMPLOYMENT CONTRACT?

Your HR department can probably provide you with an employment contract to give your new employee, but if you don't have one, you can probably find and purchase a template from an HR services company, or ask for help from your company's lawyer or legal department. Elements covered in the contract may include some of the following:

- Commencement date, term, and job location

- Position and duties

- Employee compensation

- Employee benefits

- Insurance notice (in which the company claims the right to insure the employee's life under a policy selected by the employer)

- Noncompete limitations (see left page)

- Nondisclosure agreement (see page 177) or confidentiality policy

- Statement of company ownership and protection of propriety information and inventions (including software, client list, marketing plans, etc.)

- Notice to return confidential information upon leaving company

- Nonsolicitation agreement (in which the employee agrees not to solicit, entice, or hire away the company's employees or provide information about employment terms to competitors)

- Right of employer to terminate due to discontinuance of business

- Right to terminate if the employee becomes permanently disabled

- Right to terminate with specified notice, or for employee to resign with specified notice

- Remedies for breach of confidentiality or noncompete agreement, including cause for legal action or permanent injunction

- How to modify this agreement

- Date, place, and signatures of employer and employee

Employment letters

When a letter will suffice

An alternative to a contract is an **employment letter**, or a job offer letter, which states the company's intention to hire the employee at the agreed-upon salary and other terms. It protects the new hire should you change your mind. An employment letter should specify the at-will relationship, if one exists. (This is the right of you and the employee to terminate the employement relationship at any time at your discretion; see page 93). It shouldn't specify job duration, nor list grounds for termination. When a contract is not used, the letter is often a standard part of the hiring process and most candidates will be reluctant to give notice to their current employers without it.

Send two copies to the candidate and ask him or her to sign both, keep one, and return the second one to the company.

EMPLOYMENT LETTER

Date, Year
Name
Address
Re: Terms of Employment
Dear Name,

We are delighted that you will be joining us at Widgets, Inc. This letter sets forth the terms of your employment.

You will be employed in the position of assistant sales manager and will report to the senior sales manager, Bob Jones. Your first day of employment will be on November 23. Your compensation will be a salary at the annual rate of $38,000, payable in biweekly installments. At the end of six months of employment, you will be eligible for a 10% bonus, to be based on performance and determined by your supervising manager. You will be entitled to two weeks of paid vacation for each full year of employment completed, with a maximum period of three weeks. In addition, you will be fully eligible for participation in the health and other benefit plans of the company.

Our employment relationship will be terminable at will, which means that either you or the Company may terminate your employment at any time and for any reason or for no reason with or without notice (or upon two weeks' notice for pay in lieu of notice if terminated by the Company).

By signing below, you not only accept the terms and conditions of this offer, but also represent to the Company that you are under no obligation or agreement that would prevent you from becoming an employee of the Company or adversely impact your ability to perform the expected services. This letter will contain the entire agreement and understanding between you and the Company and supersedes any prior or contemporaneous agreements, understandings, communications, offers, representations, warranties or commitments, oral or written, by or on behalf of the Company. The terms of your employment may in the future be amended, but only by a written document that is signed by both you and, on behalf of the Company, a duly authorized officer.

Please sign and date this and return by November 23, 2003, to Human Resources at Widgets, Inc.

Welcome to the company.

Sincerely,

Widgets, Inc.   Agreed and Accepted:
By: Bob Jones   John Wright

_____   _____

Title: Senior Sales Manager
Date: Nov. 16, 2003

Noncompete agreements

Protecting your company against employee exits

Most managers don't like to think about an employee's exit when they're hiring. But that's just the time to consider all the future possibilities and to make smart decisions to protect the company. Many employees will have access to sensitive proprietary data, and when they leave your company, some might be tempted to take that with them. If that information were to wind up in the hands of a competitor, it could cost your company business.

Most HR experts advise having any new employee who might have access to such proprietary information sign a **noncompete agreement** (also known as a "covenant not to compete"). In this, an employee agrees not to become an owner or employee of any business that competes with yours, for a specific period of time or in a specific location. It can also include clauses about not using proprietary information, such as software code, to create competitive products.

The noncompete can either be a separate document or as a clause in the hiring contract. If you want to use a noncompete agreement or clause, make sure it's drafted and reviewed by an attorney, and that it isn't overly ambitious in scope. Some states, like California, do not always honor noncompete agreements, but the more reasonable the time and geographic limitations, the more likely any judge is to back it up if it should ever come up in court.

If you discuss this with the employee right when he starts, and when he is signing other documents related to his new position, he will understand up front that signing the agreement is a condition of employment.

WHAT IF?

What if the employee won't sign a noncompete?

Some new hires will be reluctant to sign restrictive noncompete agreements, and in some cases it's not hard to understand why. If things don't work out, for even the most benign reasons, he or she may have to move to another state in order to find a new job! Therefore, you'll have to use your judgment. If you really want the person and you can live with a nondisclosure agreement—which most employees will have no problem signing—then go with that instead (see below). If you know up front that you absolutely cannot have your new employee work for a competitor for at least a year, then weigh the importance of having a signed noncompete agreement just as you would any other job criteria.

NONCOMPETES VS. NONDISCLOSURES

A noncompete agreement states that the employee agrees not to directly compete with you—either through his own start-up business or through an existing competitor—for a reasonable length of time and within reasonable geographic limits. A **nondisclosure agreement,** on the other hand, means the employee cannot disclose proprietary or confidential information about such things as new products, technology, finances, and business plans. The two contracts are similar in terms of the sharing of competitive data, but the nondisclosure does not restrict an employee from going to work for a competitor; it simply means that while they're employed there they won't be able to share your company's information.

Rejecting candidates

Letting candidates down gently

One oft-neglected step in the hiring process is the notification of those who didn't make the cut. Some—eager to get back to the business of business after spending a lot of time reading résumés and interviewing—will let days or weeks drift by before notifying candidates that they haven't been selected. Others never initiate the call at all.

But it's critical that you make these calls right after you hire someone. For one thing, the candidates who came in to meet with you may have figured they had a good chance of getting the position. Assuming no news is good news, they may not vigorously pursue another offer as long as they think they're still up for the position with you. So, a phone call is not only good etiquette, but good business ethics.

Keep in mind, too, that you will likely have to make additional hires in the future. And what you do on each job search reflects both on you and the company. The more responsibly you handle each one and the more good will you put out there, the better your reputation will be.

An example of what to say when rejecting a candidate might be: "Hi, Ted, this is Joe Smith from Widgets, Inc. I just wanted to let you know that we have made a decision about the management position. After reviewing all the candidates' qualifications, we've decided to offer the job to the one who most closely meets the needs of the position. We enjoyed meeting you and appreciate your interest. And I would encourage you to apply for any future openings here that match your interests and qualifications. Best of luck in your search."

Of course, don't reject anyone until you've worked out all the details with the new employee and he has signed a contract. You don't want to make your rejection calls, only to find out that your chosen candidate has changed his mind. By being courteous and respectful when rejecting other candidates, you'll ensures that if something goes awry with your current pick, you will have some other options down the road.

ASK THE EXPERTS

If the candidate asks why he wasn't chosen, should I tell him the truth?

That's a tough call and completely up to you. The truth can hurt in some cases—if, say, the candidate was just completely wrong for the job. But if you thought the candidate would have been a top pick if he only had had more training in a particular area or had a few more years experience under his belt, it won't hurt you—and could be a big help to that candidate going forward if you tell him that.

Can't I let candidates know up front that they'll hear from me only if we decide to hire them?

You can, and that would let you off the hook in terms of calling candidates who didn't make the cut. However, you run the risk of losing good candidates if the search takes longer than expected. If a few weeks go by, they may assume they didn't get the job and take another position.

Can HR call to reject candidates, or do I have to do that myself?

That's up to you. In general, if you've been the one to interview the candidates, particularly those in the final round, it's considered good etiquette to let the losers down yourself. But if the interview process wasn't that involved or competitive or if you had dozens of candidates, and it would take you days to call them all, then, by all means, delegate. Another acceptable option, in lieu of phone calls, is to send out a form letter to all the candidates.

Helpful resources

BOOKS

Compensating the Sales Force: A Practical Guide to Designing Winning Sales Compensation Plans
by David J. Cichelli

Paying for Performance: A Guide to Compensation Management (Second edition)
by Peter T. Chingos

Compensation Solution: How to Develop an Employee-Driven Rewards System
by John E. Tropman

In the Company of Owners: The Truth about Stock Options (and Why Every Employee Should Have Them)
by Joseph Blasi

101 Salary Secrets: Negotiate Like a Pro
by Daniel Porot

WEB SITES

Salary.com
www.salary.com
This comprehensive site includes compensation tips and tools for both small business owners and managers at midsize and large companies. Includes tools for comparing and analyzing existing pay practices as well as for planning pay increases and bonuses.

Workforce Management
www.workforce.com
Workforce Management magazine's web site includes articles about strategic pay, compensation budget analysis, and the use of special perks and bonuses.

CHAPTER ELEVEN

POSTHIRE: ENSURING SUCCESS

Plan out the first few weeks

Get ready for the employee's arrival before she walks in the door

Congratulations! You're excited about the great new hire you've made, and you're looking forward to welcoming her. But you still have a few things left to do to ensure that she will be able to integrate successfully with your team and begin contributing in a meaningful way.

You should spend some time planning out the first few weeks in as much detail as possible before the new employee starts so that you can communicate clearly what you expect her to be doing on a day-to-day basis and from a big-picture perspective. Consider taking the time to map out a challenging but manageable project that will take from one to three weeks to complete. Have specific goals for the project and be ready to communicate them in detail. This will allow the new employee to integrate into the culture and begin contributing right away.

Remember that she may need considerable help in the beginning getting adjusted. If you know you're not going to be available for that, you may want to assign a buddy, or sponsor, to work with that person (see page 182). But make sure to supervise the integration process so you can quickly address and correct any problems that arise.

You should also decide whether to review the employee's performance after the first month or two, and what that review will include (see page 190). For a new employee's first performance review, pay particular attention to how well she is adjusting to the company's environment, and also focus any bad habits that should be nipped in the bud.

CREATING AN EFFECTIVE ORIENTATION PROGRAM

A **buddy program**, as they're called in some organizations, can be a company's secret weapon of employee orientation. In a typical program, a manager assigns a veteran employee, or "buddy," to help train a new employee. The buddy shows the new employee the ropes for the first few days or weeks—explaining company process, answering questions, or in some cases, working with the new employee on a project. This can be a very successful set-up for both the long-term employee and the new one.

Keep in mind, however, that being a buddy isn't usually part of an employee's job. It is something you can ask or encourage, but you cannot demand it as part of the job's responsibilities. In general, it's best to make it a volunteer job; that way, you'll know that the person helping your new hire is someone who wants to be doing it and not someone who will resent you and the new person for it. In retail environments, where employees may be competing for sales commissions, you may want to offer an added incentive—an extra day of vacation or a choice overtime opportunity—to encourage an employee to sponsor a new hire.

The first day

Ways to make the employee feel at home

For new employees, the first day can be either an exciting adventure or an eight-hour exercise in confusion and frustration. And that's more or less up to you and the way you handle their arrival. An employee's first day can set the tone for their experience at your company, so you'll want to do your best to make it a good first day.

The day the employee starts, send out an announcement letter or memo to as many people as you think should be notified (see sample at top of page 185). Send it to everyone in your immediate department and then to any departments with which you work closely. Include biographical and previous work experience, but leave out personal information.

When the new hire arrives, show her around the building, rest rooms, cafeteria, vending machines, and key offices, such as HR and the technology help desk, if applicable. If you have a particularly large campus or confusing layout, you may even want to prepare a map for new hires so they can navigate easily during their first week.

At some point during the day, stop by the office or desk of each person in your department with the new employee and introduce them to each other. If the employee has an orientation at HR the first day, escort her over there. And if possible, plan to take her to lunch as well.

At the end of the first day or on the second day, sit down with the employee to talk more in depth about a new assignment you've prepared (see page 182) or about the projects your team is currently working on and how you see her fitting into them. Spend some time helping the employee to set some performance goals for that period see page 188), such as learning to use a new software program. Then, if the candidate's performance is going to be reviewed after the first few months, let her know about it and explain what the review will be evaluating (see page 190).

EMPLOYEE INTRODUCTION LETTER

I am delighted to announce that we have a new addition to our team, John Wright, who joins us as Eastern Sales Manager.

John most recently held a national sales position with Logmakers, Inc., where he personally increased sales by 34% during his three-year tenure. Prior to that success, John earned a degree in economics from Eastern University.

We know John will make a lasting and valuable contribution here at Widgets, Inc., and we wish him every success.

John's extension is 5627. Please take some time out today to introduce yourselves and to welcome him to the team.

CREATE A CLEAN, WELL-LIT SPACE

The most common culprit in first-day chaos is lack of preparation. The employee arrives on time, only to find his computer hasn't been hooked up to the network or he doesn't have a working phone. In some cases, the powers that be haven't even figured out where the new hire is going to sit, so he ends up at a temporary desk or, worse, in a chair in the hallway, waiting for someone to find a better location.

That kind of disorganization can hamper a first day and can extend through the first week, so do your best to get the logistics squared away in advance. Make sure you have an office or workstation designated, preferably the permanent space for that position, and that all the pieces—desk, chair, working telephone—are in place. Have the computer set up with the right software and have the network connections checked. Set up an e-mail account and test that as well. By preparing the environment for the new hire, you'll be going a long way toward ensuring successful integration.

Training

You may have found the perfect person for the job, but that doesn't mean he or she knows everything there is to know about the position. It's important to assess a new employee's training needs as soon as he starts and make arrangements for him to get up to speed.

If you already have a training video or other materials specifically designed for the new position, or for all people within your department, you're in good shape. You won't have to come up with training tools; you need only evaluate them periodically for their relevance. (Outdated training tools can sometimes be worse than no training at all.)

If the new hire needs special training—for example, if he needs to learn the basics of a software program you use—the solution should be fairly simple. Manufacturers of software and other kinds of technology and tools are usually happy to provide training materials—CD-ROMs, books, etc.—or may be willing to send a trainer out to your site because they want to keep your business. You can also arrange for the employee to attend relevant workshops or seminars to bone up. Just make sure you follow up with an evaluation of the employee's competency in that area after the training so you know it was effective.

It's also possible that you've been wanting to train your entire department on a specific platform, tool, or process, and this would be a great time to do it, assuming you have the money in the budget and can make a case for it strategically. The best way to do that is to tie the training needs to specific project goals of the business, both short term and long term.

ASK THE EXPERTS

I find the "trial by fire" method to be the best way to train. Can't I just expect the employee to pick things up by doing?

There are some things a savvy employee will be able to pick up just by practicing and doing—eventually. But why wait for that person to catch on? He is bound to make a lot of mistakes in the process and it will certainly take longer for him to contribute in a meaningful way. That's why a little bit of training up front is usually a wise investment.

DON'T FORGET SAFETY

Safety training for new employees is critical, as new employees are more likely to get injured on the job than veterans. They are unaccustomed to their work areas, are often less experienced, and may lack the training necessary to perform all of their job functions safely. In addition, new employees, out to prove themselves on the new job, may take more unnecessary risks. The U.S. Department of Labor **Occupational Safety & Health Administration** (OSHA) estimates that lost productivity from injuries and illnesses costs companies $60 billion each year. Because OSHA is committed to reducing that figure by at least 2 percent each year, it offers safety training materials and programs to companies that need them, particularly to those in construction, but to general business as well. Your company's insurance coverage may also require certain steps, such as half-day safety seminars. Check with your HR department to make sure your new employee receives all the relevant safety materials—and make sure he has read them by asking him a few questions about them and then having him sign them.

Setting goals

Once your new hire is familiar with the work environment, it's time to set performance goals. When the employee has his first performance appraisal (see page 190), perhaps at the end of a 30-day evaluation period, part of what you should assess is how much progress he has made toward these goals.

Setting goals with employees doesn't have to be difficult or abstract; in fact, goals should be as clear, measurable, and specific as possible. One way to simplify and demystify the goal-setting process this process is to use the "SMART" approach (see right page). Remember to keep these goals reasonable and reachable, especially for new employees.

When setting individual goals with your new hire, it's also important to consider the organization's goals and your own goals as manager. This means making sure that the new employee's individual goals support the overall aim of the organization and your department, and do not work against them or detract from the company's overall efforts.

Make sure the goal-setting discussion is a dialogue, rather than a one-sided decree. When employees feel they had a part in developing their own assignments and goals, they understand them better and work harder to achieve them. Plus, employees will often have a better idea of what it's possible to accomplish in their jobs than you will, so it pays to listen to them.

After you set goals with your employee, remember to revisit them regularly; sometimes they may need to be modified. Then revisit them again at the start of each new review period, and set new ones if needed.

THE SMART APPROACH TO GOAL-SETTING

Make sure to set goals that are:

S: Specific In describing the goal, use words that are clear and unambiguous, and not open to different interpretations by different people.

M: Measurable Set measurable goals so that you—and your employees—will know when you have reached them. Usually this is a measure of quantity (producing 50 rocking chairs per month, for example); or quality (producing at least 48 out of 50 rocking chairs with no defects).

A: Action-Oriented The first word in every goal should be a robust verb that powerfully describes the results that will be attained. These include words like "complete," "attain," "reach," "create," "build," and so on.

R: Realistic Goals must be realistic and attainable. If most employees sign on 10 new clients per month, for example, don't suddenly require them to triple that unless you know they can do it.

T: Time-bound Specify a date by which a goal must be met, whether it's three days or three months from now.

Reviewing performance

Regular appraisals are the key to good performance

Reviewing a new employee's performance after the first month or two is key to assessing how he is progressing in his work and training. They can increase productivity and employee satisfaction, too, because they help employees to understand and take responsibility for their job duties and long-term goals.

The review process is often called a **performance appraisal**. It usually requires a manager to fill out a form that assesses and rates:

Goals/objectives How much progress the employee has made toward his goals during the review period.

Competencies How well the employee demonstrates skills or behavioral characteristics that are needed to perform the job successfully.

Values How well the employee embodies the values or philosophy of your organization.

Development Plan Which skills the employee needs to develop in order to perform his current job better; how the employee can develop in order to grow within the industry or organization.

Managers then discuss the completed form with the employee during a performance appraisal meeting.

An appraisal is a lot easier to do if you set some performance goals as soon as he starts (see page 188), and a time frame for meeting them. Many companies review new employees at 30 days or 90 days, and set different goals for each period. (Some companies refer to these periods as "probationary" periods, but this can sound unnecessarily negative.)

Once you complete the initial review with the new employee, you'll then need to integrate him into your overall biannual or annual appraisal process for current employees if your company has one. At this point, you'll need to work with the employee to set new goals for the new appraisal period.

FIVE STEPS TO SUCCESSFUL APPRAISALS

1. Prepare in advance. Have a focused, interactive initial meeting with the employee to set goals and objectives based on the job description and current projects.

2. Don't wait to communicate. Your appraisals will be less daunting if you give clear, concise feedback on a regular basis, rather than waiting for the review. Employees hate to suddenly learn in their appraisal that they've been erring all along. Address negative behaviors or performance as soon as you see it.

3. Choose a neutral spot. Most employees are extremely nervous before an appraisal meeting. Having the meeting on neutral ground, like a conference room, will put them more at ease.

4. Keep records. In addition to your actual appraisal write-up, take notes at each meeting. List the objectives, as well as any concerns expressed by the employee. You likely won't remember exactly what was said and what you may need at the next review.

5. Encourage positive performance. Even negative feedback can be delivered in an encouraging way. Tell the employee you know things can easily improve with a little effort and encourage his or her progress.

Documenting performance

You may be wondering how you are supposed to remember an employee's accomplishments during the review period when you have so many other things to do. The answer is simple: Document it.

Documenting an employee's performance is much easier than it sounds. You simply create and maintain an **employee performance file**. In this, you may want to store copies of the following:

■ The employee's job description (if you have one)

■ A copy or the goals set at the start of the review period (see page 188)

■ Copies of any relevant memos or e-mails regarding the employee's performance, or any reports, commendations, or customer feedback

■ Any written feedback from you (see page 194)

It's also a good idea to include a performance log, in which you make quick notes about the employee's performance throughout the year. Note the date and the behavior you observed. It may help you stay even more focused if you write down the specific goal or job requirement to which the observation or behavior relates.

Maintaining this log shouldn't take more than a few minutes every few days, and in the long run, it will save you a lot of effort when it's time to do the performance review. Simply review the employee's file and use the notes and documents to jog your memory.

ASK THE EXPERTS

I want to be fair, but I'm confused about what to document. Do I just record my new employee's performance, or do I also record her attitude?

It's good that you're concerned about being fair; make sure you transmit this concern to your new employee so she understands how important it is to you that you document accurately. To ensure that you're being fair, always document behaviors that relate specifically to performance expectations (which you should have worked out with her at the start of each performance appraisal period). Make a note of the date, the behavior, and the performance expectation(s) to which it relates. For example, if one of her goals is to improve her efficiency in handling customer calls and you happen to her doing an exceptional job one day, make sure to note that behavior and the goal it refers to.

Always record what you see and hear and to avoid making assumptions. And above all, don't make any notations that relate to personality or attitude; address the behavior, not the person. This approach will also reduce the likelihood that an employee will respond defensively when you give feedback.

The value of feedback

Providing regular feedback is a must for a new employee, especially during the first few months. Types of feedback include praise, constructive criticism, and corrective feedback for more serious performance issues. Feedback includes both casual comments about an employee's performance and regular feedback meetings, during which you might want to give an employee the feedback in writing too.

This is where the information you've collected in the employee performance file comes in handy—you can use it to help organize your thoughts and remind you of key points. Then, to make sure the feedback is as helpful as possible, follow these "BASIC" guidelines:

B: Behavior-Based Feedback should relate to behavior, not to attitude or to personality. Focus on the employee's observable actions and talk to her about how these actions positively or negatively impact her performance and her goals.

A: ASAP—As Soon As Possible! Give the employee feedback about her performance as soon as you can—in private if the employee does not like public praise. Find—or make—the first possible opportunity to give feedback while the performance is still fresh in everyone's mind.

S: Specific Feedback must be specific. Use words that won't mean different things to your employee than they do to you. Give your employee enough information so that she understands exactly what she should continue doing or what she needs to do differently.

I: Interactive Make the feedback discussion interactive. Your employee may also have some great ideas about how she can improve her performance.

C: Consistent Ongoing feedback will help ensure that you and your employees have a consistent view of what is expected, as well as a consistent understanding of how well those expectations are being met.

A FEW MORE FEEDBACK GUIDELINES

Building on the idea that feedback needs to be BASIC, keep these additional principles in mind when you provide any type of feedback to your employees:

Tell employees in advance Take away the element of surprise by telling employees early and often that you are going to provide them with performance feedback. This is also the perfect time to tell them that you expect them to actively participate in the discussion; plus, it gives them a chance to prepare.

Address one topic at a time No matter what kind of feedback you are giving, focus on one idea at a time. This can be challenging at first, since many managers tend to think of employees in general terms as "good performers" or "poor performers," and to view all aspects of their performance within that framework. If you follow the "A" in BASIC, however, and give feedback as soon as possible, you'll find it easier to address each topic individually, as it comes up.

Keep it brief While feedback needs to be interactive, there is no value in needlessly extending discussions. Get to the point—succinctly.

FEAR NOT NEGATIVE FEEDBACK

Most managers enjoy giving praise but hate to deliver criticism because it feels confrontational and uncomfortable. But the appraisal doesn't have to take on a negative tone simply because you're addressing certain weaknesses or areas of needed improvement. Remember, this is a service to your employees as well as to your company. They can only improve and advance if they know where they are lacking, so giving them constructive criticism is actually giving them an opportunity for advancement. Focus first on the positive, the areas in which they've made strides, and then segue into the challenges.

Hiring problems

Dealing with difficulties

Sometimes unexpected hiring problems arise, such as:

The employee doesn't show up for work. It may seem odd that someone would actually resign from a previous job, sign a letter of employment, and then go missing on the first day, but it does happen. A previous employer may have thrown a salary increase into the mix to tip the balance and keep the employee with them. In any case, unless you had the person sign a formal employment contract, there isn't much you can do. And even if you could, legally coercing an employee to work for you isn't the best way to start off a new relationship. Cut your losses on this one and go back to your list of top candidates.

The new employee isn't catching on quickly enough. You knew there would be some learning on the job, but you were hoping the learning curve would be shorter. First, talk to the employee about his progress. Find out if the training you've offered is sufficient, and if not, what is lacking. And don't jump the gun. Some employers will be reluctant to sink more money into training if they're not sure the new hire is going to work out. But you've already spent the time and money to recruit this person, and you won't know if he is right for the job until you provide all the tools. If you've done all that and the employee still seems to be in over his head, you may have to pull the plug. Hiring mistakes are painful—but they only grow more painful when they drag on.

The new employee isn't fitting in. You liked the guy, but nobody else seems to. If the situation is really bad, you may have to, with some discretion, interview the other employees to find out what's behind it. They may be brooding over a breach of internal equity or some other perceived injustice. Talk to them and to your new employee. Consider taking this opportunity to plan an offsite retreat or a team-building exercise to release tension. If there's really a clash, you'll have to decide ultimately how detrimental it is to productivity.

THE LAYOFF
YOU DIDN'T KNOW ABOUT

Consider this scenario: Management gave you the okay to hire a new employee—or replace a departing one—but they neglected to tell you about the impending company-wide layoff. Now you're faced with having to lay off an employee you have just hired, since he or she will be the one without a proven record.

On the other hand, if the position for which you've just hired is critical to the company, while another position is not, you can make a case for keeping the newly hired employee. But you'll likely have to do some damage control. Layoffs tend to be scary—for the work force, anyway—and your team is likely to have formed a closer bond with a veteran employee than the new guy, so choosing a new employee over one with seniority can damage the morale of the remaining staff. As long as you can justify your decision to the staff, explaining the importance of the position you just filled, you should be able to defuse the situation.

Postmortem

Learning from hiring mistakes

With your new employee comfortably integrated into your staff, and up to speed on his job duties, it's time to review the hiring process. Evaluating your hiring practices post-hire is key to being a good manager. Eventually you'll have to hire again and you want to be able to repeat the steps you took that worked to find the right person. And, naturally, you also want to avoid repeating the mistakes.

Start by asking yourself about the recruiting process. Did you get the most valuable candidates on the first round or did you have to tweak the job description or requirements several times? Were most of the candidates appropriate for the position or did you have to do a lot of weeding? Were they in the right salary range?

Then look at the various methods you used to advertise and recruit, and see which ones yielded the most promising prospects. If you advertised in the local paper, but all of your top picks came from a recruiter, that should tell you something. Likewise, if traditional recruiting efforts were fruitless but your own networking turned up the top three, it's worth noting this for next time.

Examine your internal processes. If you used a panel interview, did the various interviewers work well together? If the candidate was interviewed by several managers or colleagues, how smoothly did that go?

Don't overlook the valuable insight you can get from your new hire. Remember, he has just been through your company's hiring process. Was it more or less a pleasant experience? Were there any bumps in the process that he thinks you should iron out? Anything that could have potentially turned him off? The newly hired employee may feel vulnerable and reluctant to deliver negative feedback. Explain that the information is completely confidential and will not be used for any other purpose. Let him know you really value the feedback and that it will save you and the company time and money in the future.

ASK THE EXPERTS

We eked out a good hire this time, but most candidates said we didn't offer a competitive enough salary. Should I be worried about future hires?

If most of your candidates thought your package wasn't up to par, you probably should be concerned. But if you are in the position of having to convince upper management to up the salary for a certain position, you need evidence to support the claim. Get current data on salary ranges in your area and make a list of the candidates who commented on the salary. You can also circle the applicants' salary requirements and turn in the batch of résumés as tangible proof.

Helpful resources

Tools you can use

BOOKS

Creative New Employee Orientation Programs: Best Practices, Creative Ideas, and Activities for Energizing Your Orientation Program
by Doris M. Sims

New Employee Orientation: A Practical Guide for Supervisors
by Charles M. Cadwell and Michael G. Crisp (editor)

Retreats That Work: Designing and Conducting Effective Offsites for Groups and Organizations
by Sheila Campbell and Merianne Liteman

Successful New Employee Orientation: Assess, Plan, Conduct, & Evaluate Your Program
by Jean Barbazette

Performance Appraisal Question and Answer Book: A Survival Guide for Managers
by Dick C. Grote and Richard C. Grote

WEB SITES

Occupational Safety & Health Administration
www.OSHA.gov
The U.S. Department of Labor's safety site is a virtual A-to-Z on safety within the corporation.

The Performance Management & Appraisal Help Center
www.performance-appraisals.org
A free resource center for managers to get tips, tools, and the "perfect phrases" for performance appraisals.

Deliver the Promise
www.orientation.deliverthe promise.com
This web site offers help with both employee orientation program development as well as with training sessions.

All 4 One Adventures & Teambuilding
www.all4oneadventures.com/ Teambuilding.htm
This San Diego company offers off-site team-building adventures and boot camps custom-designed for corporations across the U.S.

Accel-Team
www.accelteam.com/team_ building
Team-building exercises and materials are for sale at this U.K. company's Web site.

CHAPTER TWELVE

CONTINGENCY HIRING

What is it?

And when is it right for you?

Unless it's part of the corporate culture, many managers simply overlook the option of not hiring a full-time employee. Yet, on closer inspection, the position for which they're hiring might be more appropriate for a part-time worker—or **contingency worker**, the latest term for one of those within the full gamut of part-time employees.

While the majority of part-time staff tend to fill positions in administrative or clerical positions—approximately 35 percent, according to the latest U.S. Bureau of Labor statistics—they also help out in a range of other positions, including laborer, marketing assistant, technician, and service associate. Even more experienced professionals are being hired on a per diem or project basis to create staffing flexibility and save on perks and benefits. According to the American Staffing Association, daily employment for temporary help services has increased at an average rate of 10 percent per year over the past seven years.

And it's not that surprising given how the changing business landscape is forcing companies to stay as agile and nimble as possible. When it's the right fit, contingency hiring offers companies two significant benefits: flexibility and cost-savings. Once you hire a full-time employee, you're making a long-term commitment to that position and to that employee. You can't decide a few months from now that the project that employee was working on isn't going to benefit the company's bottom line after all and you no longer need that skill set. Faced with those situations, managers will usually shuffle the employee around to other areas where he may—or may not—be needed. But temporary or part time help allows managers to gauge the success of a project before making the full-time commitment.

Temporary or contract help can also allow companies to better and more seamlessly adjust to changes in demand. If the economy sours and sales dip, you can scale down in size without having to go through a painful layoff.

ON THE OTHER HAND:
THE DOWNSIDES

Training

Any new employee who walks into your company fresh, whether full time, part time or temporary, will need training in your specific operations and way of doing business. You'll have to spend time and money getting him up to speed, and when he walks out the door, that training and intellectual capital goes with him.

Hidden costs

While you don't have to give this person benefits, a temp can often end up costing more per hour than a full-time employee. In cases of temp workers, you'll also likely pay fees to staffing firms. If the project should grow or end up taking much more time than planned, you could end up spending a big chunk of money.

Cultural issues

If the contingency worker is going to be working with your full-time people, you may have to deal with power struggles and other disruptive conflicts. For example, employers may not appreciate an outsider coming in and behaving like the expert.

FIRST PERSON INSIGHTS
A fresh approach

"Two years ago, we embarked on a massive data-consolidation project. We knew it would require many hours, and we didn't quite have all the skills in-house, so we were thinking of hiring someone. We didn't consider the possibility of a temporary hire, so we went a bit backward, starting from the conclusion of hiring a full-time person and then figuring out how that person's skills would fit into our group full time. Fortunately, we realized about halfway into the hiring process that while it was a very important job, it wasn't a permanent need. We ended up contracting the work to a very talented temporary worker and got the job done by the deadline."

Paul D., Chicago, IL

Your options

Once you decide a contingency worker is right for the position, you need to figure out which option best suits your need.

Part-time help. These hires are best suited for work that is steady, but not enough to keep someone busy for 40 hours a week. The payroll and benefits costs are lower for part-time employees, and they may have only restricted eligibility for other benefits, such as sick leave, holiday pay, and pension plan participation. You also create a flexible work environment so that if a valued full-time employee has to go part time, for personal reasons, and his or her job is one that can be shared, you can hire another part-time employee to make up the hours.

Temps. Temp work has traditionally been used for very short-term and clerical positions, such as covering for a receptionist while he's out sick or filling in for an administrative assistant on vacation. But experienced, skilled **temporary workers** are also being used for longer projects in technical fields, such as computer programming and engineering. A temp can also be a "project employee," hired for a specific short- or long-term project, and remaining just for the duration of the project. There are important differences between temp employees and independent contractors (see page 205). On the downside, because temps know they're not in it for the long haul, they have less incentive to learn the ins and outs of the company and to try to fit in with the culture.

Outsourcing. Also known as managed services, **outsourcing** means letting a provider firm handle an entire departmental function, such as payroll. By doing this, you don't have to hire anyone, but you do have to establish a relationship with the vendor and stay on top of the work they are doing, since you won't have nearly as much control as you would if the work were being done in-house. Small businesses, for example, will often outsource certain HR functions, such as payroll or benefits administration, rather than staffing up internally.

INDEPENDENT CONTRACTORS

The job of an **independent contractor** can appear similar to that of a temp, but the differences between the two are important for your company and its legal obligations. (See page 210 for more on correct classification.)

An independent contractor is someone to whom you contract specific services for a set period of time. Some examples are: a consultant you hire to help your business develop a strategy, a freelance writer you contract for your magazine, or a Webmaster who gets your site up and running. Independent contractors are great alternatives to full-time employees, since they presumably offer solid expertise without having to be integrated into the staff or offered any full-time benefits.

Depending on the business area, however, they can be pricey, so do the math before deciding. And as with any employee, make sure you get references and samples to back up any claims.

Staffing firms

Seek out specialists

While you could recruit and hire a contingent worker, it would probably take up nearly as much of your time as it would to hire a full-time employee, and with so many staffing firms out there to do the screening (and the paperwork) for you, it's not really necessary.

True, you'll pay a bit more if you use a staffing firm; the worker who would normally get $6 an hour, for example, will probably cost you $8 or $9 an hour. But for short-term projects, particularly when you're pressed for time, you can really benefit from the screening and training provided by the agency.

Since you'll be turning over a fairly important part of the process to an outside agency, make sure you choose the right firm, one that attracts the best temporary and part-time candidates out there. Start with any staffing firms you or your company have already worked with or have a relationship with. Many handle both temporary and full-time employment, so if you've had success with a recruiter in the past, you may find they can help you with other staffing needs, and you may get a price break.

If you haven't used a staffing firm in the past, use your networking contacts to find the good ones. Talk to colleagues in other departments or people you know and trust in the industry. Check with your area's chamber of commerce, since the more reputable firms will be listed.

Seek out firms that specialize in your industry and schedule a few phone conversations to find out about their experience, expertise, and services. Find out how they prequalify candidates and whether they do background checks. Don't make any deals without an in-person visit to make sure you are dealing with a professional operation. And make sure your contracts are worded so that the burden of responsibility for the employee falls on the agency and not your company.

ASK THE EXPERTS

Will the staffing firm train workers in advance of coming to us?

Some firms do offer training to their temp staffers; some don't. Find out if the company does have a training program, because that will give you a clue as to the caliber of candidates you'll see.

If the person they send me doesn't work out, will they automatically send another?

That should be part of your negotiation, although it's fairly common to have that sort of guarantee, at least for the first employee or two. Consider the first failure a fluke—and be sure to tell your staffing contact exactly what the problem was—but if you are unhappy with the caliber of talent after two or more hires, try a different firm.

A FEW TIPS FOR NEGOTIATING

- If you have to train employees for a long-term project, find out if you can do so without having to pay for their time.

- If you think you may have other staffing needs in the near future, see if you can get some sort of package deal now.

- Find out if the agency offers guarantees, waiving fees for employees who don't work out.

- If you are considering temp-to-hire, get that settled with the agency up front, as some have policies on that; you also want to make sure they bring you temp candidates who have an interest in going full time at some point.

- Make sure the agency has client references you can call.

Part of the family

Creating and maintaining a culture of camaraderie and cooperation among full-time employees is one of the biggest challenges any
manager or business owner faces. This is why integrating temps is a
kind of double challenge. They are not going to be around permanently—yet they have to be a part of the team to enhance, rather than
impede, productivity. The presence of temps can create a feeling of
instability that can in turn make full-timers edgy, so you need to anticipate those issues before they arise.

For example, if your company doesn't already have a hybrid workforce where temps are part of the culture (and often referred to as
"extended family"), then be up front and explain to your staff why
you're bringing in a temporary worker, exactly what he or she will be
doing, and for how long. If necessary, and reassure your employees that
they are not in competition with this person for their jobs. If you are
considering a temp-to-hire situation (see page 209), then consider letting employees in on that. Tell them it's experimental right now, but if it
works out, you may hire the person. That way they have a context for
meeting and working with the person coming in.

You also want to make sure you're creating a pleasant work environment for your temp. Like you would with any new hire, make sure a
workstation is available ahead of their arrival and that all the necessary
equipment is working. Treat the temp as a member of the group as
much as possible; he or she will then be more likely to be emotionally
invested in your company and the work.

ASK THE EXPERTS

Should I invite temps to company picnics and other events?

Absolutely, unless you have some strategic reason for not having them there. Corporate social events are an opportunity for employees to bond and become more comfortable with one another. You can only benefit from having your temps feel at home.

What if my other employees aren't getting along with the temp?

Talk to a couple of your employees to find out what's going on. By now you should trust their judgment, and if they're having a problem, it may be something you don't know about but should. Or you may find out it's simply insecurity among the ranks, and you just need to clarify your message to them about your temp strategy. ·

A BRIDGE TO FULL-TIME EMPLOYMENT

The **temp-to-perm arrangement** is fast becoming a popular way to hire full time. And temps think so too; according to the American Staffing Association, 74 percent of temporary employees consider temp work as a way to get a permanent job, rather than an end in itself. If you're not positive from the outset that you want to hire, the temp-to-hire is a win-win. You get the advantage of a trial period in which you can see how the employee fits in, in addition to getting the temporary project done, while not having to commit to anything long term.

Legal issues

Avoiding the pitfalls

It's easy to think that by not hiring full-time help, you avoid the legal hassles that come with new hires. But, in fact, you're just faced with different legal issues, and it's important to get them straight before you bring someone on.

Classification, for example, is a big one. Companies and their managers can get into trouble by failing to fully understand the difference between employees and independent contractors. Caught misclassifying a worker, they may later be forced to pay both the company's share and the worker's share of contributions to Social Security and Medicare, plus any income tax that would have been withheld, including federal unemployment tax.

Classification can get confusing, particularly in a world of telecommuting employees and virtual offices. Technically, the difference between an employee and an independent contractor is that an independent contractor can control not only the outcome of the project but also the means of accomplishing it—in other words, when and how he does it. (In fact, in testing for employee status, the IRS looks at the amount of control you have over the worker's time and means for doing the work.) An independent contractor is typically not entitled to worker's compensation, unemployment, overtime, health insurance or other benefits, and he usually works offsite with his own equipment.

The important thing to remember is that while it may be very clear to you what the status of the independent contractor is, it needs to be abundantly clear in the wording of your contract (see page 211). It's a good idea to have one standard agreement that you use for all contractors working on the same kinds of projects or in the same department, and have any new draft reviewed by an attorney.

ASK THE EXPERTS

Can the independent contractor work onsite and still be considered independent?

In some cases, the contractor will have to work on-site. A technician hired to fix a problem with your network will have to go wherever the network equipment is. So that alone is not evidence of an employer-employee relationship.

ANATOMY OF THE CONTRACT

The following is a short list of elements that should appear in an agreement with an independent contractor. This can be used as a guide, but have an attorney look over any document you plan to use.

Services to be performed. This section should list, in as much detail as necessary, what you are hiring the contractor to do. This is also necessary to protect you in the event that the work is unsatisfactory.

Time frame. Set a deadline and make it clear it isn't an indefinite arrangement.

Compensation. This should include the terms of payment and agreed-upon price, whether per hour of work or fee based, as well as how invoices should be submitted.

Status of independent contractor. This is a paragraph stating clearly that you, as the company, are employing this person to be an independent contractor, and not an employee for any purposes. It states that the contractor will have complete control over how the work is done. You may also add a section specifying that the contractor will supply all of his own equipment and tools.

Ownership rights. In the case of freelance work for a publishing company, you need to specify the kind of rights your company has to the finished material (e.g., whether you can use it in other media formats or in promotional material).

Helpful resources

Tools you can use

BOOKS

Responsible Restructuring: Creative and Profitable Alternatives to Layoffs
by Wayne F. Cascio

Healing the Wounds: Overcoming the Trauma of Layoffs and Revitalizing Downsized Organizations
by David M. Noer

Retaining Top Employees
by J. Leslie McKeown

WEB SITES

The Center for Hospitality Research at Cornell University
www.hotelschool.cornell.edu/chr/research
Visit this site for a copy of their study, "How to Compare Apples to Oranges: Balancing Internal Candidates' Job-Performance Data with External Candidates' Selection-Test Results," by Michael C. Sturman, Ph.D., Robin A. Cheramie, and Luke H. Cashen.

Peopleclick
www.peopleclick.com/solutions/erp.asp
Check out Peopleclick's Employee Referral Manager, designed to help companies run an employee referral program that maximizes participation and produces more and better candidates.

EXAMPLES OF CURRENT EMPLOYEE REFERRAL PROGRAMS

SRI International
www.sri.com/jobs/referral.html
SRI International, formerly the Stanford Research Institute, is an independent, non-profit research institute that conducts client-supported research and development for government agencies, commercial businesses, and nonprofit foundations.

North Shore Bank
www.northshorebank.com/AUs/Careers/EmpRefProg.asp
This program at a Wisconsin community bank claims success with its ERP.

Glossary

At-will relationship A legal term describing the relationship between an employee and an employer; it means the employee is hired at the will of the employer and may be terminated at the discretion of the employer.

Behavior-based question An interview question about a candidate's prior job experiences that aims to reveal if the candidate has the specific skills and knowledge to perform particular job functions.

Bona fide occupational qualification An exception to a discrimination rule that allows an employer to hire someone based on an otherwise illegal criterion, such as religious preference.

Buddy program A new employee orientation program in which an existing and usually veteran employee is assigned to train the new employee.

Classification The way in which various types of part-time employees and contractors are legally defined, which ensures that the employer pays all required benefits for them.

Character defamation This is the legal term for the situation in which a candidate believes a reference has told a prospective employer something falsely negative about him or her; it can be the basis for a lawsuit.

Compensation package Salary and other incentives, such as a bonus, 401(k), and other perks, which have monetary value and are thus part of an employee's total compensation.

Contingency worker An employee who works part time or on a contract or temporary basis, rather than full time.

Cost-per-hire The total cost associated with hiring divided by the number of full-time hires made in a given period.

Counteroffer A salary increase, promotion, or other incentive a current employer extends to retain an employee who has received a job offer at another company.

Credit check An investigation into a prospective employee's financial history via his or her credit report.

Diversity recruiting Proactively recruiting candidates from a range of minority groups in order to create a more diverse work force.

Echoing An interview technique in which the interviewer repeats part of the candidate's previous answer in order to prompt him or her to elaborate.

EEOC The Equal Employment Opportunity Commission is the government agency that enforces federal workplace discrimination (EEO) laws.

Employee referral program (ERP) A corporate program that offers cash or other incentives to current employees if they refer a qualified applicant who is subsequently hired.

Employment contract A formal agreement between a company and the new hire that outlines the employee's salary and other compensation, date of hire, job duties, and other employment particulars. Once signed and dated by both employer and employee, it becomes a legal document. *See also* employment letter.

Employment inquiry release form A form the candidate signs that makes it legal for the prospective employer to do a background check on him or her.

Employment letter Similar to an employment contract, this outlines a new hire's job duties, compensation, and other benefits in the form of a letter. It should not include the job duration or grounds for termination. *See also* employment contract.

Exempt employee An employee, usually full time, who works for an annual salary, is exempt from earning overtime pay, and is eligible for company benefits such as health insurance, vacation, etc. *See also* nonexempt employee.

Handheld personal digital assistant An electronic all-in-one personal organizer, such as a Palm Pilot.

Headhunter An agency or professional to whom companies outsource the task of recruiting talent. *See also* Recruiter.

High-probability hire Used to describe a hire with the greatest likelihood of succeeding and staying long term at your organization.

Independent contractor or freelancer A skilled professional contracted to work, usually part time, for a set duration or when called upon. They do not typically work inhouse and do not need to be integrated into the workplace staff.

Job application A structured form that candidates fill out to apply for the position that allows hiring managers to see the same information about all applicants.

Job board A Web site that allows job seekers to post their resumes online for prospective employers to find.

Job book A binder of job opportunities, kept at a college's career center, which students use to find out about summer jobs, internships, and full- and part-time positions.

Job criteria A list of skills or qualifications demanded by a position, such as a certain educational level or previous employment experience.

Job description A concise but thorough overview of a job'vvs responsibilities.

Job fair A recruiting fair sponsored by local colleges or technical schools, in which dozens of employers set up informational booths, allowing job seekers to shop for jobs.

Job functions A list of a position's responsibilities and duties.

Keyword A word used as a reference point for finding other words or information, usually online.

Noncompete limitation A clause in an employment contract that prevents an employee from using a company's proprietary, confidential information if he or she goes to work for a competitor after leaving the current company.

Noncompete agreement Also known as a "covenant not to compete," this is a clause in the employment contract, or separate legal agreement, which states that, after leaving the current employer, the employee cannot become the owner or employee of any business that competes with the current employer for a specified period of time.

Nondisclosure agreement A clause in an employment contract that prevents an employee from disclosing proprietary or confidential corporate information, such as information about products, clients, or finances.

Nonexempt employee An employee who works for an hourly wage, is not exempt from earning overtime pay, and is not eligible for most company benefits, such as health insurance, vacation, etc. *See also* exempt employee.

Nonverbal cues The revealing body language displayed by a candidate during an interview.

Occupational Safety and Health Administration (OSHA) A division of the U.S. Department of Labor that promotes safety in the workplace and focuses on limiting injuries on the job.

Outsourcing Contracting out an entire departmental function to a firm that specializes in that function, such as payroll or benefits administration. Also known as managed services.

Panel or group interview An interview in which the candidate faces a panel of three or more interviewers who each ask their own questions.

Performance bonus A cash or other type of bonus given to an employee at some designated point if the employee performs exceptionally well.

Performance appraisal A formal review of an employee's performance at a predetermined time; this usually requires the employer and sometimes the employee to fill in a form appraising and rating the employee's performance. Also known as a performance review.

Personality-based question An interview question that reveals aspects of a candidate's personality.

Personnel database A corporate database of employee resumes.

Pre-interview reference checking The process of checking some resume information, such as educational level or previous job titles, before deciding to interview in person.

Postmortem Reviewing the hiring process after it has been completed to evaluate how well it was executed and to make any necessary improvements.

Qualified privilege The legal right of former employers to pass on appropriate, truthful information about a candidate to a prospective employer.

Recruiter An agency or professional to whom companies outsource the task of recruiting talent. See also Headhunter.

Redeployment program An internal corporate program that helps laid-off employees find positions in other departments in the company.

Reference checking Calling a candidate's former employers or colleagues to double-check their skills, experience, workplace attitude, and level of productivity.

Reasonable accommodations As defined by the Americans with Disabilities Act, this requires employers to make a reasonable effort to accommodate the physical or mental limitations of an otherwise qualified applicant or employee who happens to have a disability.

Retainer A regular monthly fee paid to engage the services of a recruiting firm over an agreed-upon period of time.

Salary cap The highest possible salary that will be paid for a position.

Search engine An Internet tool, such as Google or Yahoo!, that allows users to search the Web for key words.

Signing bonus An up-front cash incentive offered as part of a new employee's compensation package if he or she accepts the offer of employment.

Skills or proficiency test A standardized test used to objectively assess a candidate's ability to perform certain job tasks, such as typing or proofreading.

Stress interview An interview in which the interviewer asks the candidate hostile or confrontational questions in order to test the candidate's ability to handle stressful workplace situations.

Sync To synchronize information from two sources, such as a PC desktop calendar and a handheld digital device.

Telecommuting When a full-time or contract employee works offsite or from home, usually using the Internet to send work or to connect to the employer's internal network.

Temp-to-perm arrangement When a temporary work agreement effectively serves as a trial employment period, and can later lead to permanent hire status.

Temporary employee A temporary employee hired on an hourly basis or for a set fee to complete a short-term project in-house or to work onsite for a set duration. Also known as a project worker.

Turnover rate The rate at which a company's employees leave or are terminated.

Videoconferencing A technology tool that allows people in different locations, such as an interviewer and a candidate, to talk and view each other via video.

Virtual fair An online simulation of a traditional job fair in which employers list job openings and provide information about their companies.

Weighting skills Assigning a numerical value to each skill or qualification required for a job, then evaluating how well potential hires fill those qualifications.

Index

About the author

C.J. Prince is the Executive Editor of *CEO Magazine* and the author of dozens of articles about the hiring process and business strategy and management. She also writes a monthly column about small-business management for *Entrepreneur Magazine*. She lives in New York City.

Barnes & Noble would like to thank the following consultants for their help in preparing this book: **Ruth K. Robbins** of Career Momentum/Résumés Plus in New York City, and a certified counselor of the Five O'Clock Club; and **Colleen Stewart**, who has been in executive recruiting for over 14 years and is currently a Recruiting Manager at Georgia Pacific Corporation in Atlanta.

Barnes & Noble Management Basics™
Barbara J. Morgan Publisher
Barb Chintz Editorial Director, Barnes & Noble Basics
Leonard Vigliarolo Design Director
Wynn Madrigal Senior Editor
Leslie Stem Design Assistant
Emily Seese Editorial Assistant
Della R. Mancuso Production Manager

Illustrations by Barton Stabler/ARTVILLE